ANDALUS:
SPAIN UNDER THE MUSLIMS

The Giralda at Seville

ANDALUS: SPAIN UNDER THE MUSLIMS

by

EDWYN HOLE, c.b.e.,
Late H.M. Consul General in the Levant Service
Author of "Syrian Harvest"

ILLUSTRATED

London
Robert Hale Limited
63 Old Brompton Road, S.W.7

B 58 -15991

Printed in Great Britain by Richard Clay and Company, Ltd.,
Bungay, Suffolk

To

JUAN TEMBOURY

IN GRATITUDE AND AFFECTION

PRAISE TO GOD, WHO ORDAINED THAT WHOSO SPEAKETH WITH PRIDE OF AL-ANDALUS MAY DO SO WITHOUT FEAR AND AS BOLDLY AS PLEASETH HIM, NOR MEET ANY THAT MAY GAINSAY HIM OR DISTURB HIM IN HIS PURPOSE. FOR THE DAY MAY NOT BE CALLED DARK, AND A LOVELY FACE MAY NOT BE TERMED UGLY.

AL-SHAQUNDI, "OF THE EXCELLENCY OF ANDALUS."

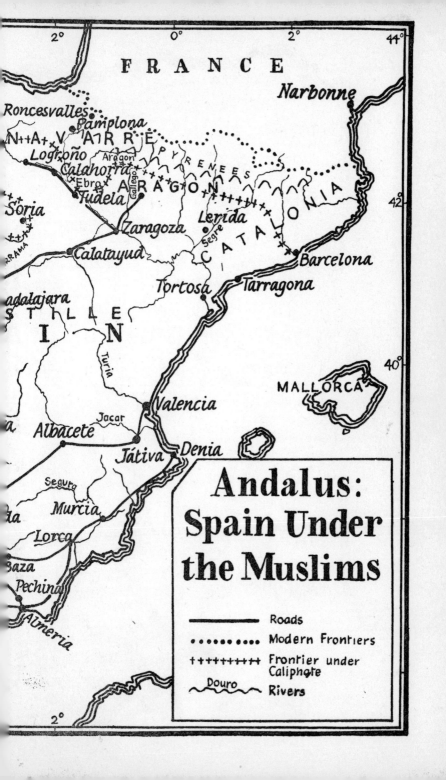

Andalus: Spain Under the Muslims

———————	Roads
••••••••••	Modern Frontiers
+++++++++	Frontier under Caliphate
‿‿‿ Douro	Rivers

CONTENTS

LIST OF ILLUSTRATIONS

the Wise in the second half of the 13th century. Although the scenes were painted on the Christian side of the frontier, the artist was familiar with Muslim costume. Each Canticle faced a page divided into six pictures, each with its caption above it in the Galician dialect. In this illustration from the 28th Cantiga the Sultan appears in the top left-hand corner, wearing eastern dress but attended by a bodyguard in Christian armour. In the foreground is a ballista being wound up by a mixed team of Moors and Christian mercenaries, the latter wearing armour of overlapping scales: two Moors use their typical shields to protect their backs.

PREFACE

Few historical periods of comparable interest and importance have been so neglected by English scholars as the seven centuries of Muslim rule in Spain.

The only full-length study that I have been able to trace is James Cavanagh Murphy's *The History of the Mahometan Empire in Spain*, which was published in 1816. The *Cambridge Mediaeval History* so artfully conceals its chapter on the Western Caliphate that it eluded me the last time I was at the British Museum Reading Room: I have since learned from a Spanish bibliography that it occupies pages 400 to 442 in the third volume, and is signed "R. Altamira", though written by Angel Gonzalez Palencia. In Previté Orton's summary of the *C. M. H.*, which runs to twelve hundred odd pages, rather less than seven are allotted to those seven centuries.

In other countries the subject has been treated more worthily: first by a Dutchman, Reinhart Dozy, who wrote all but a hundred years ago; in Spain by a dynasty of Arabists, the "*banu Codera*", Ribera, Asin, Garcia Gomez and others; in France Pérès and Lévi-Provençal. These were my guides in that unfamiliar but fascinating country, and my aim in this book is to lure the English reader along the same paths and pass on to him some of the pleasure and interest I have myself derived from the study.

My thanks are due first to the scholars I have mentioned, in particular to Professor Emilio García Gomez, who was kind enough to read the book in proof and acquit me of any major error; to Juan Temboury Alvarez, the Commissioner of Fine Arts in Malaga, who introduced me to the Caliphate of Cordoba and made me free of his splendid library; and to Gamel and Gerald Brenan, whose home at Churriana was as the shadow of a great rock in a sometimes weary land. I must also acknowledge my debt to those who have provided me with the illustrations; the Victoria and Albert Museum for Nos. 16 and 17, the Spanish National Tourist Office for the frontispiece and Nos. 1, 2, 3, 4, 9 and 10, Ampliaciones Mas for Nos. 6, 7, 11, 12, 14 and 15.

E.H.

Malaga,
  April 1957.

CHAPTER ONE

HISTORY

AL-ANDALUS was the name by which the Arabs knew that
part of Spain which they ruled from the 8th till the 15th century:
its modern form of Andalusia denotes the eight southern provinces which make up the command of a Capitan-General,
resident at Granada.   It is a rough triangle lying between the
Sierra Morena and the Mediterranean: it includes the most
varied natural features, ranging from the rich lowlands of the
Guadalquivir basin to the mountains that fringe the southern
coast, some of which, in the Sierra Nevada, are crowned with
eternal snow, while at their foot sugar-cane is cultivated in a
subtropical belt.

The Arabs accounted it one of the five earthly paradises.
The legend runs that when Allah was busied with the creation
and dealing out good and evil to the newborn countries, each
of which was given five wishes, Andalus asked for a clear sky, a
beautiful sea full of fishes, ripe fruit and fair women, all of which
were permitted, but the fifth wish, for good government, was
refused, for that would have made a Heaven on earth, which
could not be countenanced.

The origin of the name is uncertain: some have derived it
from Vandalitia or Vandalucia, alleged to mean the home of
the Vandals, but others deny that these names ever existed, and
class that derivation with such schoolboy etymology as seeks the
origin of "saunter", for example, in "Sainte Terre", because a
footsore palmer returning from the Holy Land would make
slow progress.   There is no obvious reason why Arabs should
drop an initial v or w which they had no trouble in pronouncing, though it cannot be denied that they had nothing against a
bit of *Volksetymologie* if it fitted in with their theories.   Witness
the story they concocted round the Roman name of Hispania,
which they applied to the whole peninsula, as opposed to their
own territory of Andalus. Ishban, they opined, was the
founder of that kingdom, flourishing shortly after the Flood, but
after prospering for a season the people fell into Magian heresies
and their depravity offended God, wherefore he withheld the
rain, and the springs sank into the earth, and the country became desert for a hundred years.   Then certain peoples from
North Africa were brought there by one Batrik, who landed at

Cadiz and built a capital at Italica, and after a hundred and
fifty-seven years Romans under a second Ishban, the son of
Titosh, brought the land to a high pitch of efficiency and conquered Jerusalem. Where could one find more perspicuous evidence of the truth of this than in the history of the precious
Table of Sulayman, which Ishban brought back from Jerusalem
and the Arabs found at Toledo, all solid gold and plastered with
jewels? Tarik it was that found it, but his general Musa
wrested it from him, though Tarik tore off one leg and brought
it out before the Caliph, when Musa claimed credit for the
victory, so proving him a liar.

It is a pleasing story, containing just enough truth to set one
off on unprofitable speculation, for Titus did sack Jerusalem,
and Vespasian though not his son was at least his father. And
the Arabic "Ishban" might stand for either Hispania or
Vespasianus, both of them barbarous words with which a high-
born Arab would want as little truck as possible. But I look
forward to meeting someone proficient in the Berber tongue,
whom I shall ask whether Andalus was not the name which the
Berbers gave to the country they saw looming across the narrow
seas.

The history of the colonization of the country by the Celt-
Iberians, Phoenicians, Greeks, Carthaginians, Romans and
Visigoths is happily outside the scope of this book. Its
frontiers were never fixed: in the first surge of conquest at the
beginning of the 8th century the Muslims pushed as far as the
southern skirts of the mountains that frame the northern seaboard of Spain; only the Asturias held out under Pelayo, to
whom history or legend ascribes a victory at Covadonga in 722.
To-day a monastery occupies the grotto where his scanty
followers defied the invaders. The Arab chroniclers made
light of the affair: "a wild ass", they relate, "reared up against
the Muslims; they defeated his army time and again, till nothing remained of it but thirty men and two women, and these
lived on the wild honey that they found in clefts of the rocks.
At last the Muslims wearied of them and would not be bothered
longer, saying, 'What harm can thirty wild asses do us?'"
This was nevertheless the turn of the tide and the beginning of
the Reconquista, which was to be protracted for seven and a
half centuries, until the fall of Granada, the last Muslim citadel
in Spain.

The Muslim conquest began as a light-hearted reconnaissance from North Africa. The Governor, Musa ibn
Nusair, sent one Tarik with a handful of Berbers to raid and

report; Tarik met with amazing success; all resistance crumbled in one battle on the Guadalete. The Goths were hopelessly divided: certain princely commanders, claiming to have a better right to the kingdom than the elected king Roderic, deserted on the field of battle; the Bishop of Seville, brother of the late king, fought on the Muslim side; and the little Berber force went through the country as if it were butter. Apart from a few Gothic magnates (who hastened to come to terms), none of the population had much to lose by a change of masters; Muslim rule was lighter, and their taxes less oppressive. The large Jewish community in particular, who made up perhaps a third of the population,[1] had everything to gain. A generation earlier, there had been a Jewish revival in North Africa, during which many Berber tribes, who could never resist a new creed, had embraced Judaism; and the oppressed Jews in Spain, encouraged by this accession of strength, had concerted a revolt with their brethren in Africa. It was a failure, and the Goths had exacted a heavy penalty. The entire community was reduced to slavery: the young children were taken to be brought up as Christians, and Jews were forbidden to marry among themselves. Little wonder that they threw in their lot with the invaders, who on their side were glad to have their support and set them to garrison the towns behind them as they pressed forward.

So easy was the victory and so great the booty that Tarik ignored Musa's orders and pushed on to the Gothic capital at Toledo; Musa, furious with jealousy at his success, hurried after him in a series of forced marches, and when he came up and Tarik advanced to receive him with due honours, slashed him across the face with his whip. Musa in his turn did not escape the jealousy of the Caliph at Damascus, who recalled him, stripped him of his wealth and honours and was with difficulty persuaded to leave him his life.

The ease of the victory so puzzled later chroniclers that they invented the legend of Count Julian to explain it. This was the Gothic governor of Ceuta [2] who sent his daughter to Roderic to be brought up in his court and given the polish only to be acquired in great houses. Roderic found the young beauty to his taste and took advantage of her. When Julian came to fetch her away, Roderic, believing him unaware of his daughter's misadventure, asked him to send him some falcons for hunting,

[1] Hadrian is said to have transported to Spain forty thousand families of the tribe of Judah and ten thousand of the tribe of Benjamin.

[2] Later research makes Julian a Berber named Ulban.

and Julian replied that he would send him such and so many as
he could never imagine. He then took his revenge by advising
Tarik on the best line of attack.   The Berber troops were the
promised falcons.

.   .   .   .   .

To conquer was child's play, to govern somewhat harder.
One *wali* succeeded another in Andalus, each using his brief
years of survival to look for fresh fields for pillage in the
Christian north.   New waves of conquest swirled past Pelayo's
fastness deep into France, as far as Poitiers, where Charles
Martel at last broke the invaders, preserving Europe from
Muslim domination and putting an end to Musa's ambitious
dream of marching back to Syria through Southern Europe and
Asia Minor.

The next quarter of a century was a ferment of insurrections,
religious upheavals and civil wars on both sides of the straits.
Then came a lull: Andalus was ruled by Yusuf al-Fikri, who
had been chosen by a coalition of chieftains sick of civil commotion, and in ten years or so had reduced the country to some
sort of discipline.   At the other end of the Mediterranean the
Abbasid dynasty had ousted the Umayyads and set about the
methodical extermination of their line.   One Abd al-Rahman
of the royal blood escaped by a hair's breadth from the massacre
of his family, made his way by a series of miracles across Egypt
and North Africa, both strongly held by his enemies, and from
a precarious retreat at Sabra sent his freedman Badr across to
Spain, to find out what prospect there was of his clansmen
offering him shelter.   At this point his ambitions were modest,
and Yusuf would have found them easy to satisfy, but some
trifle put him out, and he chose to fight.   The end of it was that
Abd al-Rahman was proclaimed Amir of Cordoba (756) and
founded a dynasty that endured till the end of the 10th century
and was a centre of light and leading in Europe.

Like all oriental kingdoms it had its ups and downs, corresponding to the temper of its rulers.   A strong hand and quick
decision were needed to keep the unruly subjects in check.
The pure-bred Arabs formed an aristocracy that distracted the
Peninsula with all their old tribal feuds, and exasperated the
country-bred with their arrogance.   The Berbers, who had
been the spearhead of the invasion, were undisciplined head-
strong savages, prone to bouts of religious mania; the far more
numerous native population were Christians, though a great
number had embraced Islam for the privileges it carried: the

old noble Gothic families were still powerful and kept an almost royal state. Those that remained faithful to Christianity were by no means reduced to serfdom, but kept their independence, so long as they paid their poll-tax. The Arabs had few race prejudices, and intermarriage was the rule; they found the fair northern women very much to their liking, the Umayyad Amirs in particular: so that most of the royal house had fair hair and blue eyes, and the language spoken in the palace was the dialect of Galicia.

The regime was tolerant beyond all contemporary standards, but when a curb was needed, it was applied ruthlessly, and the annals of the Amirate are deeply stained with murder, treachery and massacre. So soon as a ruler faltered, rebellion broke out on all sides: in the lean years between 852 and 912, when one weak Amir followed another, most of the country was ruled by three country-born clans, the Banu Qasi on the northern marches, the Banu Merwan in the west, and ibn Hafsun in the south. All their chiefs were *muwallads*, Spaniards born whose forefathers had turned Muslim: the last, while professing Islam, remained secretly a Christian. But for a century before and another afterwards there were strong men at Cordoba, who ruled a kingdom that was culturally and militarily centuries in advance of its neighbours.

To keep their turbulent subjects in hand, Abd al-Rahman and his successors found it necessary to reinforce their native talents, however outstanding, by a standing army of mercenaries, mostly recruited from slaves, bought from Jewish traders. These were chiefly Slavs: the two words are synonymous in Andalus. Their freeborn subjects were no less liable to military service in time of need, but when the harvest was ready or they thought the campaign had lasted long enough, they were apt to melt away. The country was rarely at peace; the frontier in the north was always aflame or smouldering: it was not a stable line but a wide area of desolation, into which Muslim or Christian princes led their armies, whenever peace at home left their hands free for adventure. Later, as the Christian kingdoms gathered strength, they built castles at strategic points and gradually extended their hold around these bases: this was the birth of Castille—the Castles. As yet there was no national inspiration for the perennial campaigning, only the love of loot or the simple relish of a good fight.

One Abd al-Rahman founded the Amirate, Abd al-Rahman al-Dakhil, the Immigrant: it reached its zenith under another, Abd al-Rahman al-Nasir l'il-Din Allah, the Victorious in the

Faith. He reigned for nearly half a century (912–961) and threw off the last figment of obedience to faraway Bagdad, assuming the title of Caliph and appointing the great mosque at Cordoba to serve as a substitute for Mecca. He imposed himself on the Christian kings as arbiter of their destinies, and received with appropriate dignity their contending embassies, often the kings themselves, bending their stiff necks to the rigid protocol of the Caliph's court. Yet when al-Nasir died, they found a writing in which, reviewing his long and glorious reign, he could not call to mind more than fourteen days of unclouded happiness.

Al-Nasir's son Hakam II, after maintaining the prestige of the Caliphate for the sixteen years of his reign, appointed Hisham, the son of his old age, to succeed him, but it was one of his chamberlains that took his place, Abu Amir Muhammad al-Mansur, an Arab of noble but poor family, who won the favour of Hisham's mother, the Basque Aurora or Subh, and came to rule first in Hisham's name and then in his own. He became famous all over Europe under the name of Almanzor, harrying the Christian kingdoms during his twenty-six years of dictatorship as never before, thrusting as far as the Galician shrine of Sant'Iago of Compostella, the tomb of the champion of Spain and the root of Christian endeavour. Before him no Muslim army had ever advanced so far; Mansur demolished all but the grave itself, which he respected because an old monk met him there and showed no fear.

After Mansur and his son Mudhaffar, the Caliphate foundered in civil war and mob violence. Al-Nasir's palace at al-Zahra was sacked and its treasures pillaged, the Empire split into as many fragments as there were fortified towns and castles that could accommodate an ephemeral court. The 11th century was the age of the Taifas—a score or so of little principalities, where in the intervals between wars the arts were cultivated in city states that foreshadowed the Italian republics but lacked their political vigour. Scholars, craftsmen and musicians were encouraged by fantastic rewards: the princes themselves condescended to woo the Muses, science, astronomy, music, but all alike professed literature. Since the precepts of Islam put the representational arts outside the pale, no intellectual outlet remained but eloquence, so that it was always expected of any leading citizen that he should be able to express his thoughts and aspirations—even his ultimatums—with delicacy and precision in verse or at least rhymed prose. It was an extremely artificial medium—Garcia Gomez has

described it as algebraical—in which all the princes laid claim
to proficiency, one of them, Mu'tamid of Seville, ranking with
the best Arab poets of all time.

While these little potentates postured in the light and
warmth, strutting in their delightful palaces, where all was
culture and elegance and courtesy (though the background was
heavy with foul play and double-dealing), a painful *dénouement*
was drawing near.   On both frontiers peoples incapable of
respecting their aesthetic distinction were moving brutally
forward.   In the Maghrib a new empire was growing, based as
always on a fresh explosion of religious fervour, which had
produced the Almoravids—*al-murabbitun*, warriors for the faith
—a Muslim counterpart of the Christian fighting orders.
Drawn from the wild tribes that came swarming up from the
ends of the Sahara in the middle of the 11th century, they had
been forged by Yusuf ibn Tashufin into an irresistible instrument of conquest: so that by 1080 he ruled from his new red
capital of Marrakesh most of the vast expanse of north-west
Africa.

In Spain meantime the Christian kings were taking their
first halting steps towards the unity without which the *Reconquista* was inconceivable.   Monarchies were taking shape, rival
kingdoms coming together.   At the end of the 10th century,
shortly before the Caliphate went down, Sancho el Mayor,
King of Navarre and married to the sister of the Count of
Castille, had taken advantage of the confusion following the
murder of his brother-in-law to assume the overlordship of
Castille, installing his son Fernando as his vassal.   Fernando in
turn added the kingdoms of Leon and Galicia to his dominions,
assuming the proud title of Emperor of the Spains.   He maintained relentless pressure on the Muslim bulwark of Toledo,
and was strong enough to make a *promenade militaire* through the
Muslim countries and extort homage and tribute from the
weak and contentious princelings.   When he died in 1062,
custom divided his realm between his three sons, but Alfonso
VI, to whom Leon fell, took up the crusade where his father left
it.   The Muslims were content to keep their state at the
expense of a doubled tribute, and it was only the fall of Toledo
in 1085 that opened their eyes to the imminent danger.   They
turned for help to Yusuf ibn Tashufin, the rising star of the
Maghrib, and it seemed the foreordained defender of Islam.
Yusuf came, and with his disciplined armies, trained to move as
one man to the roll of the drums, inflicted a heavy defeat on
Alfonso at Sagrajas near Badajoz, but receiving the news of his

son's death the same day went back to Africa to deal with domestic troubles. When renewed Christian pressure brought him back to Spain four years later, he applied himself to reducing the Taifas one by one and founding the Almoravid empire. The fair spring of love and poetry never came to summer: one by one the lights went out; Mu'tamid wrote his best poetry in exile and misery.

The Almoravids, predominantly Berber or negro and redoubtable fighting men, were despised as untutored savages by their cultured subjects, who derived what consolation they could from sneering at their ungentlemanly inability to appreciate good verse. However, their flaming puritanism soon succumbed to the fleshpots of Andalusia, and within two generations the Muslim dominions were weaker and worse governed than before Yusuf came to defend them.

Then came a new revival in the Maghrib, and they were in their turn ousted by the Almohads—al-muwahhidun or unitarians —more fanatical if possible, and certainly not more enlightened. The rise of this sect reads like a wild flight of fancy. One ibn Tumart set up as a Mahdi—a sort of Muslim Messiah—and acquired the reputation of a holy man. The Berbers of a village in the Atlas Mountains called Tinmalal invited him to take up his dwelling among them: it had long been a summer billet for the Fatimid Caliph's Frank and Rumi slaves, and in the course of time the good folk of Tinmalal had acquired a colouring fair beyond the ordinary. Ibn Tumart accepted the invitation, took in at a glance the natural strength of the position and the unpardonable blond complexion of the natives. He built a mosque outside the village and invited the men to its consecration, during which they were massacred by his adherents. He then occupied the village and maintained himself there for twenty years, though frequently besieged and at last heavily defeated. He was succeeded by a remarkable Berber called Abd al-Mu'min, who assumed his mantle in 1130 and in a reign of thirty years pushed his frontiers as far as Egypt.[1]

---

[1] Another story of ibn Tumart's methods comes straight out of the Arabian Nights. A succession of reverses giving rise to doubts of the authenticity of his mission, he resolved on a miracle to confirm the faith of his followers, and concerted with one Wansherishi to bring it about. This man accordingly drifted into the community, dirty and apparently half-witted, and played the part for some months until he acquired the status of village idiot. Then one morning he appeared well dressed and perfumed and expounding the Quran like a faqih. He explained that an

The Almohads like their predecessors were completely captivated by Spain: their princes took wives from the daughters of ibn Mardanish (Martinez), one of the Spanish families that had turned Muslim: they adorned Seville with the Giralda, which still stands guard by the cathedral, but the Christians have added a stupid revolving saint on top; they became fervent patrons of bull-fighting and introduced the Spanish breed in the Maghrib.

Meanwhile Christian Spain was making painful progress towards unity of command, through long years of combinations, alliances and betrayals. One medium of consolidation was a series of royal marriages within prohibited degrees, which were duly annulled but the offspring legitimated. From this confusion emerged another Alfonso, the first king of Aragon of that name, known to history as the Fighter, el Batallador. He had taken Zaragoza, the key of the northern marches, in 1118 and inflicted a heavy defeat on the Almoravids in 1120. In 1126 he reunited the kingdoms held by his grandfather Alfonso VI of Castille. He died without issue, but his brother Ramiro, who had taken orders, was brought out from his cell long enough to marry and provide for the succession: his infant daughter was married off in the manner of those times to the Count of Barcelona, so uniting Catalonia and Aragon, and Ramiro having discharged his responsibilities went back to his cell.

A further step towards unity was taken in 1135, when Alfonso VII, the grandson of Alfonso VI, was crowned with great pomp as Emperor of the Spains and King of the Two Religions, in the presence of the rulers of Navarre and Catalonia and certain Muslim princes. Alfonso regarded himself as the feudal overlord of the whole peninsula, with vassals both Christian and Muslim, but his conception of empire died with him and was followed by another generation of confusion and internecine war. The long reign of Alfonso VIII of Castille

---

angel had washed his heart and inspired him in a single pentecostal moment with an intimate knowledge of the scriptures. He claimed moreover by divine guidance to know who would go to Paradise and who not, recommending that the latter should at once be killed off. In support of his assertions he called in evidence certain angels at the bottom of a well (accomplices whom he had posted there) who duly confirmed the truth of his mission. A well with such holy associations must evidently not be profaned by secular use, so he had it at once filled in with boulders, afterwards passing the villagers in review and executing those from whom he anticipated opposition.

affords a measure of continuity: after initial victories over the Almoravids, he met with a stunning reverse at Alarcos (1195) at the hands of the Almohads, due largely to the inopportune desertion of his allies. The Almohads had however shot their bolt, and the victory had no lasting effect. Alfonso chastised his peccant allies at leisure and strengthened his bonds with Leon by the classic expedient of marrying his daughter to her first cousin.

At the end of his long reign he reaped the harvest of his patient scheming: the Almohads were finally crushed in what under his leadership had assumed the dimensions of a crusade: Castille, Leon, Aragon, Navarre and even Portugal (independent since 1143) all took part in the great victory of Navas de Tolosa in 1212, victory so complete that half a million Muslims emigrated to Africa, and a few years later an Almohad prince was on his knees to Alfonso for help to regain a footing in the Maghrib. The Almohad prince who suffered the defeat abdicated at once and drank himself to death.

Fernando III, grandson of Alfonso VIII, whom a kind fairy had endowed with a clever and persuasive mother and the good luck to live during a period of sweet reasonableness, made the best use of the coalition over which he presided. Seville fell to him in 1236, Cordoba in 1248: his allies of Aragon and Barcelona accounted for Valencia, Murcia and the Balearic Islands, and a few years after his death little remained to the Muslims but the tributary kingdom of Granada and a string of ports on the south coast.

The end of the Reconquest was in sight, but it was delayed for two more centuries by the chronic inability of Christian rulers to agree. It was not till the marriage of Fernando II of Aragon and Isabel of Castille finally united Spain that a full-scale operation could be undertaken. The royal consorts built a stone-walled camp at Santa Fé, a few miles south of Granada, whence they directed the siege for ten years. Five hundred years earlier, in similar circumstances, the great Caliph had built the city called al-Fath—Conquest—at the gates of Toledo. Isabel's drive and brilliant choice of generals won the day, and with the fall of Granada in 1492 the long Muslim domination of Andalusia came to an end.

· · · · ·

It is a trite saying, customarily reinforced by appeal to a poet who deserves better, that East is East and West is West and never the twain shall meet: and as inaccurate as most of the *clichés* that nowadays pass for wit. Kipling's East and West were geographical abstractions, and the poem from which the line was torn recounts how on at least one occasion East and West did meet and fraternize in the persons of worthy representatives. East and West have inevitably been coming into collision ever since the peoples began to migrate, first in intermittent waves out of Asia, some of which on arrival in Europe dissolved into a confused eddy, as with the Goths; more often they kept their momentum and pushed the earlier populations to the Atlantic fringes. The eastward movements, less frequent, had less of the blind urge that drives hosts of lemmings to drown themselves in the Atlantic: they were deliberate and planned: Rome mounted an offensive to relieve pressure on her eastern frontier: Europe took the cross to free the Holy Land: Don John of Austria and Admiral Codrington led their navies against the Osmanli.

Trade also supplied a motive as compelling: it has been argued a little fantastically but with much truth that the discovery of America was a by-product of European dyspepsia, the object of explorers from Marco Polo onwards being the quest of spices to render mediaeval cooking endurable. Historians have often over-estimated the religious motive, for although the clash of Christendom and Islam was genuine enough during the crusades, kings and popes found it a convenient screen for purposes quite as urgent but less respectable, and as this became apparent it lost its drive. Whatever the motives, these conflicts brought about contacts, relatively short-lived, between East and West, which had an abiding influence on the West and to some extent affected the East. There have been many later opportunities of mutual instruction: the latest is the discovery of oil in the Middle East, where the incidence of western methods and the rain of gold are importing a new and perilous ferment.

In the past these contacts were rarely more than superficial; in most fields eastern and western civilizations impinged but did not penetrate. What lends interest to the tangled history of Spain is their intimate interpenetration over a period of centuries. Wars and the names of kings are a handy peg on which to hang history, but history itself is composed not so much of events as of the slow growth and flowering of peoples in their everyday lives; and in Spain there was no field of activity, however improbable it might seem, in which Christian and Muslim did not live and move together. Even war did not divide them, as might seem inevitable, along the cleavage of religion; Muslims are constantly found allied with Christians

against Christians allied with other Muslims; Christians join
in Muslim feuds and fight under the Umayyad standard:
Christians living in Andalus turn out against the Christian in-
vader, and there are always warriors of either faith ready to
follow the highest bidder. The most familiar example is the
life-story of the Cid.

In times of peace the Christian kings affected Muslim dress
and sent their sons to be taught manners in the court of Cordoba: they married their daughters to Muslim princes, and
the brides adopted Islam with the approval of both families.
The Muslim king of Seville gave his daughter as concubine to
his enemy Alfonso, who baptized her Isabel and had by her his
only son, Sancho. Elsewhere in Europe, apart from Norman
Sicily, intermarriage was exceptional: once during the crusades
a treaty was being negotiated between Saladin and Richard
Lionheart, to be sealed by the wedding of Richard's widowed
sister Joanna and one of Saladin's brothers, but nothing came of
it: perhaps it was frowned on as an invention of the Angevin
family devil; but in Spain it was common form. In matters of
statecraft the court of the Amirs was accepted by all as the most
enlightened in the Peninsula, and the kings turned to it for
guidance on delicate issues. The best medical advice also is
available there, and Sancho the Fat, King of Leon, sweated his
way to Cordoba to be treated by the Caliph's Jewish physician,
who indeed relieved him of some of his burden.

At a lower level, there was the same absence of religious
bigotry: it can be aroused, and easily, but Muslim and Christian live together, speak one another's language and give their
children one another's names, and so long as the Christian
pays his taxes and refrains from insulting the Prophet, he is left
free to practise his religion under the rule of his bishop. In
contrast to the practice in other Muslim countries, new churches
are allowed to be built up to the fall of the Caliphate, and the
bells call the congregation to worship. In the Byzantine
Empire, on the other hand, Christian Greeks denied this privilege to Christian Armenians, and it is not much more than a
century since it was given to Catholics in England. The
Muslims indeed took an ingenuous pleasure in attending the
more splendid Christian celebrations, and were frequent visitors at the monasteries, joining heartily in the copious feasts of
the name-day. There are echoes of this tolerant or indifferent
attitude from the other side of the frontier: Alfonso the Wise
made a collection of *Cantigas*—canticles, often narrative—one
of which related how a King of Morocco won a battle by the aid

of the Blessed Virgin's standard, while another tells of Her
intervention on behalf of a Muslim woman and her infant
daughter.

The Christians had an additional motive for such enlightened
tolerance; the Muslim was an admirable craftsman and content with modest wages; moreover when the frontier was
pushed southward, they were hard put to it to people the new
territory, and Muslim workmen and farm hands were at a
premium. All over Christian Spain Mudejar [1] architects and
masons have left their mark in towers and steeples: the
cathedral treasures are full of their handiwork. When he was
dying, the great fighting bishop of Toledo, Rodrigo Jimenes de
Roda, left orders that he was to be shrouded in a certain
Moorish tissue, which is to-day one of the glories of the collection of the Marques de Cerralbo.

The Christians of Andalus came to be called Mozarabes, a
corruption of the Arabic word *musta'rib*, which means a person
affecting Arab ways or passing for an Arab. They dressed like
Arabs and found that for conversation and such delicate *genres*
as love-poems Arabic was a far more supple medium than their
own rude Romance tongue. Archbishops denounce the unworthy practice and bewail the lack of clerks with a command
of Latin, but all to no effect: and the Mozarabe rite in the
Arabic tongue is still read in certain cathedral chapels. As a
rule the Christians were content with their lot, except for a
while in Cordoba, when many sought martyrdom by publicly
blaspheming against the Prophet; and they did not emigrate
to the neighbouring Christian countries until the fanatical
Almoravids made their life a burden. Then at last convoys of
Mozarabes followed Alfonso's army across the frontier.

That the Caliph of Cordoba kept the most sumptuous and
civilized court in Spain is sufficiently established, though in
Spain itself this was so completely forgotten that the sites of the
palaces were lost. A century or so ago, when the history of the
Muslim domination began to be a subject of research, students
whose romantic admiration outstripped their intellectual
equipment discovered in it the origin of most of the culture and
institutions of modern Europe. Medicine, natural science,
philosophy, music, Gothic architecture, epic and lyric poetry,
textiles, mathematics, everything was traced back to that
magical hothouse. Reaction was inevitable; fresh documents
came to light, students with a better knowledge of Arabic
redeciphered the inscriptions; and as research was conducted

[1] The word means a Muslim resident in the Christian areas.

more scientifically, the soundness of some of the hypotheses was questioned, along with the competence of some of their authors.

The tide of "debunking" has ebbed, and the nineteen hundreds have seen the growth in Spain of a pleiad of talented Arabic scholars, ably seconded by French specialists in North Africa, whose patient and frequently inspired work has immensely increased knowledge of the period. On the whole their work has gone far towards redressing the balance and establishing on a foundation of solid scholarship many of the romantic speculations of their predecessors.

CHAPTER TWO

THE CAPITAL

THE FOUNDATION of Cordoba is lost in the mists of pre-history. Modern speculation assigns it a Phoenician origin and makes of it a sister-city of that elusive Tartessus. The settlement was probably destroyed and rebuilt more than once in its early days: ibn Bashkuwal has preserved a hint of such a rebirth in his legend of the king of near-by Almodovar, who went hunting and lost his favourite hawk in thick cover; searching for her he had his slaves cut away the matted brush-wood, and so came on wondrous foundations; on which he set about building a city to be worthy of them. The story may not be so far from the truth: towns have been lost in this way; even Abd al-Rahman's palace-city of al-Zahra a few miles from the capital has only recently been unearthed.

Even in the bronze age the natives seem to have been dis-tinguished artists: the Museum shows with pardonable com-placency a bell-shaped cup of such advanced craftsmanship as hardly to be credited to that distant era.

Little is known of Cordoba's history before the second century B.C.; it must already have been a considerable township when the Romans took it, for almost at once they established there the first *colonia* outside of Italy. It had an immediate vogue: so many Romans of good family settled there that it was given the title of Patrician; by which the Arabs used to set great store, and the present-day inhabitants no less.

In Roman times the province produced its share of great men —Trajan, Hadrian, Lucan, the Senecas—and the Cordobans earned the compliments of Cicero himself by the purity of their Latin. Later on, it was Bishop Osio of Cordoba who converted the Emperor Constantine to Christianity and drafted the Nicene Creed.[1]

Under the Umayyads the town covered a far greater area than now; there were suburbs that extended for miles both west and east, and where the palaces of al-Zahra and al-Zahira attracted agglomerations that afforded all the conveniences of

---

[1] Cordoba also prides itself on being the birth-place of Gonzalo Fern-andez, the *Gran Capitan*, and the poet Gongora, besides a number of poets and painters whose names are less familiar to English ears, and three of the finest toreros known to history.

independent towns.   Al-Shaqundi says that he rode through
ten miles of uninterrupted buildings, along a road lit by lamps
from end to end.   On the north too, towards the Sierra, the
plain was embroidered with hamlets and country mansions;
while across the bridge, nestling in the loop of the river, was the
Shaqunda suburb,[1] which was the focus of a revolt that nearly
cost the first Hakam his throne and life.   When the rebels had
made such progress that they threatened the palace, he first
curled and scented his hair, so that if he was killed, they would
recognize the body and give him fitting burial, and then led a
charge on the insurgents.   While thus occupying their attention, he sent his servants to set fire to their homes, and when
they hurried to save them, fell on their rear and cut them to
pieces.   To discourage further revolts, he banished all the
surviving inhabitants;   they went to found new quarters abroad;
in Fez, where their name still endures, and in Alexandria, where
for ten years they made themselves so obnoxious that the Caliph
Ma'mun had to come to terms and convey them to the island
of Crete, which belonged to his neighbour the Emperor of Rum.
There they set up as pirates, and for a century or more were a
thorn in the side of the Byzantines.[2]

After expelling the uneasy inhabitants of Shaqunda, Hakam
razed the suburb to the ground and forbade that it should ever
be rebuilt—a prohibition that was respected to the end of the
Caliphate.

.   .   .   .   .

Cordoba has a very distinct personality: two poets have
sought to crystallize it in a word; Lorca called it "*lejana y sola*"
—distant and aloof: Manuel Machado in his "Cante Hondo"
caught its essence more truly with "*Romana y Mora, Cordoba*

---

[1] Possibly the heir of the Roman suburb of Secunda, so called from the
second mile-stone on the southern road.

[2] The end of their career makes an attractive story.   It seems that the
Emperor of Rum sent an embassy to their chief, Abd al-Aziz ibn Habib,
offering him twice the revenue he derived from his operations, if he would
conduct himself with more consideration for his neighbours.   He accepted,
and relations improved.   Then Romanus sent him five hundred mares,
begging him to take care of them, as a drought had burnt up all the
pasture in Byzantium, and assigning to him in return for this service, all
the fillies they might produce.   To this also he agreed.   Then after a
certain time, the Emperor sent five hundred soldiers under Nicephorus the
Domestic, who landed one night, seized the stables, mounted the mares, and
utterly destroyed that kingdom.

callada".[1]   The Cordobans indeed rate highly their Roman and
Moorish beginnings, and the town has a perceptible reserve
and reticence: not flaunting its charms but yielding them up to
such as take pains to seek them out.   Too many visitors, after
conscientiously "doing" the Mosque and taking a photograph
of the bridge and Calahorra, drive on with easy minds, never
suspecting the beauties lurking round corners in the winding
Muslim streets: the church doors and façades of old patrician
mansions tucked away in narrow lanes and crooked little *plazas*:
lovely patios with orange-trees and roses and myrtle, framed in
rejas designed to reveal while protecting their secluded charm:
the *compases*, which are gardens not enclosed within the house but
lying between it and the street, guarded by platoons of flower-
pots: balconies which contribute their quota of blossoms at
every level: bodegas, some of which have trellised patios which
provide a typical setting for that *cante hondo* on which the
Cordobans pride themselves so whole-heartedly.   There you
may listen to *cantadores* singing to the accompaniment of the
guitar *serranas* and *fandangos* and *verdiales* and a host of other
varieties only to be distinguished by the very knowledgeable.
The mode is oriental and falls strangely on untutored ears; but
sitting in the warm evening calm of the patio, richly scented
with orange blossom or *damas de noche*, and supported by a few
instructive glasses of amber Montilla, even an English listener
may find his pulses stirring.

   Many visitors miss much of the authentic *bouquet* of Cordoba,
deluded by the heavy type of the guide-books into the belief that
the city lives in its past: the glory of the great Mosque (which
is indeed unique) blinds them to the vivid life that mantles in
the *barrios* and in particular to the Santa Marina *barrio*, where
the Caliphate of the 10th century pales its ineffectual fires before that of the 19th and 20th, when Guerrita succeeded Lagar-
tijo, and Manolete outshone both of them.   These three *toreros*
are the Cordobans' crowning glory: in their style (if I may
trust a member of the Spanish Royal Academy), the spirit of
the city is incarnate: "that stoicism so illustriously professed by
Seneca, himself a native of Cordoba, that impassibility in face
of the ineluctable, that sobriety and avoidance of the super-
fluous, as essential in the bull-ring as in the palestra".   Wherefore a very learned gentleman and an absolute authority on the
antiquities of Cordoba did not fail to indicate *en passant* a two-
storied house at the foot of al-Zahra where a famous *torero* had
retired: and the enlightened Town Council included in the

[1] "Silent Cordoba, Roman and Moorish."

Museum of Crafts and Folklore which it created recently at the
Zoco in the old Jewish quarter, a substantial section concerned
with the life and death of Manolete, down to the hide of the
bull, which by some unpredictable reflex killed that perfect
master of the ring.

.   .   .   .   .

The Cathedral Mosque, a miracle above all the mosques of
the Levant, was built and enlarged by masters who brought no
less than genius to the solution of their problems. The first was
that fundamental problem of architecture, of putting a roof
over a large area: here it was done by borrowing the short
Roman columns that were available, setting a heavy capital on
top to carry a thicker pillar, from which springs the arch that
carried the roof. The structure is stiffened by horse-shoe arches
based on the lower capitals. The success of this treatment is at
once apparent, when from the Patio de los Naranjos one passes
through the Puerta de las Palmas and gets one's first view of
the twilight beauty of the interior, with its infinite expanse and
long-drawn vistas in every direction; the architects have
achieved an effect of mystery and serenity, in which the alter-
nate red and yellow of the dowels of the arches, so far from
jarring, add a note of warmth and welcome. On the last night
of Ramadan, when all the lamps were lit and the scent of aloes
and amber eddied in the aisles, the grandeur of Islam was
plainly manifest.

The successive enlargements of the mosque by Abd al-
Rahman II, Hakam II and Mansur all respected the original
method and did no worse than widen the frame. Even the
interpolation of the Christian Cathedral in the 16th century was
less calamitous than it might have been: a casual eye might not
notice its interference with the vast and airy perspective of the
aisles. However much Charles V may have regretted his
unreflecting permission for the work to proceed, it was a cheap
ransom to pay for the preservation of the rest of the lovely
structure.

Hakam's lavish embellishments gave his architect two more
opportunities to excel, in building the vaulted lanterns that
give additional light over the first bay of the new central aisle
(now part of the Villaviciosa chapel), and those immediately
in front of the *mihrab*, which he did without breaking the
orderly procession of the columns by the insertion of piers.
Both problems were solved brilliantly: the architect did without
piers by stiffening the arches with interposed cross-members in

the form of a richly ornamented x. He also invented a masterly treatment of the dome, using semi-circular arches which intersect in such a manner that they leave the centre free. He seems to have enjoyed the intellectual exercise so much that he presented three variants of the solution.

The cupola of the *mihrab* is a graceful shell-form that anticipates English Georgian design by eight hundred years: there is disagreement about it: certain guide-books assert that it is carved from a single block of marble, but Torres Balbas says somewhat disappointingly that it is stucco, and so indeed it appears. But Don Rafael Castejon, who knows more about the antiquities of Cordoba than anyone, assured me that in fact it is a single block, and the stucco is no more than a skin applied by restorers in the last century. He also demolished the story that the last aisle is a later addition, by pointing out that below the floor of the mosque each column stands on an isolated foundation of masonry, and this is equally true of the last row of columns, which would all be carried on a continuous foundation, if they replaced an outer wall.

The mosaic inscriptions and decorations of the *mihrab* arch are very beautiful: they are the work of Byzantine artists using materials the gift of Nicephorus Phocas. Only the central five *voussoirs* of the *mihrab* arch and the upper half of the screen with its inscription are the original work: the lower half is a restoration, and the Kufic characters are meaningless. The arch on the right was executed by local craftsmen, who were formed by the Byzantine masters: that on the left had to be reconstituted in modern times, and is the work of mosaicists from Valencia.

The dome of the *mihrab* is marked at its base by a lovely curved line, broken regularly by cusps, in glazed earthenware. Don Rafael Castejon spoke of it as unique, though it must have been made in Spain. He mourned his failure to trace its provenance: nothing like it has ever come to light.

Hakam's improvements included the demolition of the old ablution tanks, which had to be filled from jars brought by mules, and the piping of water to four great cisterns that he had cut out of the living rock of the Sierra and drawn to the city along a road built exclusively to that end. Each of them required the massed power of seventy of the strongest oxen. To bring water to his subjects was one of the noblest gifts a Sultan could make; his father before him had built a twenty-mile aqueduct to bring water into the city, to a fountain called the Naura, where it discharged into a vast tank which was

presided over by an enigmatic group of statuary, consisting of
a huge golden lion with jewelled eyes, perpetually watered by
a gigantic fuller.

The orientation of the mosque is faulty, the *qibla* almost due
south; a consequence perhaps of the original partition of the
Christian church, accepted by Syrian architects, familiar with
the bearing of the *qibla* in their own country. Hakam was
fully aware of the error, and on the day after his father's funeral,
he assembled the Council of State, and put the question whether
he ought to destroy the whole fabric and build a new mosque
with the correct aspect. They answered that Allah so far from
expressing dissatisfaction had consistently encouraged its
founders with victories; wherefore no change was called for.

The Great Mosque was always a centre of religious activity of
the most conservative stamp. Throughout the history of
Muslim Spain, the ruler had to reckon with the *faqihs*—the
jurists and professional theologians. "In the old time", says
al-Shaqundi, "Cordoba was the seat of empire, the centre of
science, the beacon of religion, the abode of nobility and leadership. The inhabitants had deep respect for the Law and com-
peted for the primacy in this science: and the kings humbled
themselves before the doctors, exalting their station and acting
in accordance with their opinions." These doctors belonged
to the rigid school of Malik ibn Anas, which from the first
asserted its authority in the person of Yahya ibn Yahya, a
Berber who had sat at Malik's feet and was so strongly en-
trenched that he could set the people to publicly insulting the
Amir, and openly incite them to revolt: yet when Hakam put
an end to that rebellion with fire and sword, he dared not
punish Yahya, but confirmed him in his post of qadi.

Once established, the Maliki doctors saw to it that no more
liberal doctrine should get a hearing: it was their practice to
turn the mob on to sacking any rival teacher's house and burning his library: in this manner they prevailed against ibn
Masarra and ibn Qulaib, who professed a measure of free will
obnoxious to the Malikis. During the reigns of the Caliphs
Abd al-Rahman and Hakam the influence of the *faqihs* was
insignificant, but the usurper Mansur had to manœuvre for
their support and lend a hand with the destruction of the philosophical works in Hakam's peerless library.[1] The kings of the

[1] Hakam's library is said to have contained four hundred thousand books
and manuscripts. Four hundred years later, King Charles the Wise of
France designing to adorn his capital with a library could only lay his
hands on nine hundred books, of which six hundred treated of theology.

Taifas ignored them, but they came into their own again under the Almoravids, gratifying Yusuf al-Tashufin with a *fetwa* that the Taifa kings were dissolute and must be put down. In return Yusuf sent orders to the governors of provinces to burn all books, the Quran alone excepted, which would seem a sufficient guarantee of orthodoxy; but when the Almohads followed on, they found to their horror that the *faqihs* were giving opinions based on Malik's derived practice, and not, as they should, on the *ipsissima verba* of the Quran. Wherefore they sent shiploads of Maliki books to pious bonfires at Fez.

In due course the Christians also took a hand at book-burning: Cardinal Cisneros, to whom Ferdinand and Isabella entrusted the conversion of the Granada Muslims, burnt thousands in the Bibirambla square: and ten years later the Holy Office getting into its stride set about burning the Moriscos together with their books.[1]

The jealous labours of the *faqihs* however failed to repress the intellectual flowering of Andalus; the rich and cultured aristocracy of Cordoba persisted in the pursuit of learning, and even in the study of rival systems. An account of the intellectual achievements of the Caliphate would call for a more ambitious book than this; it would be easy—but demoralizing to the general reader—to list a score of Spanish–Arabic authors —poets, historians, philosophers, physicians, mystics, mathematicians—whose names are household words wherever Arabic literature is studied. There were indeed many whose direct influence on European scholarship made them familiar to mediaeval students, usually under odd travesties of their names: Avenpace, Averroes, Avicebron, Abulcasi, Avenzoar, Maimonides. It was through the Western Caliphate that Greek scholarship filtered into Europe; and it was perhaps the religious obligation of making the pilgrimage at least once in a

---

[1] The pious practice endured into the 17th century. Ribera tells of a collection of Arabic books in the Escurial, formed chiefly by the capture of certain shiploads belonging to Muley Zidan. The Moroccan Emperor sent an embassy to ask for their return, and the matter being referred to the Holy Office the Inquisitor, after a wistful reference to Cisneros's practice, showed his tolerance by consenting to the return of books on geography and science, but not religious works, as they might fortify the might of Islam. His view being submitted to the Council of State, the majority voted to burn the lot, only a small minority following the Inquisitor. As so often happens, neither majority nor minority had its way; for on the enlightened advice of the Marques de Velada, the King locked them all up out of harm's way.

lifetime that most stimulated and encouraged the revival of learning. Those who undertook the costly and perilous journey to the Holy Places often spent years travelling and studying in the eastern lands of Islam, with the object of bringing back knowledge and wisdom to enhance the title of *Hajj* which they had so painfully earned.

In fact there was a universal and boundless desire for instruction. When a Byzantine Emperor sent as a gift to Abd al-Rahman III a manuscript of Dioscorides' "Materia Medica" which nobody could read, the Caliph asked the Emperor for a Greek interpreter, and when after its long double journey across Europe the embassy brought him back, the Caliph's Jewish physician and ambassador convened the entire College of Physicians to collaborate in deciphering and translating the precious work. Abd al-Rahman's son Hakam, himself a great scholar, took an active part in the pursuit of learning, sending his agents abroad to seek out and purchase manuscripts, and inviting scholars to his court, where he treated them sumptuously. Spain became a powerful magnet on which foreign *savants* converged.

Learning took an oddly roundabout road from Athens to Cordoba. In the 5th century the orthodox Councils of Byzantium persecuted the Nestorians and at last roundly branded them heretical; they withdrew further and further from the capital until the embattled orthodox synod expelled them from their last refuge at Edessa. They struck east across the frontier to Nisibin, where they were welcomed by the Sassanid rulers of Persia, and given a home in Jundeshapur in the southwest provinces. A great medical school grew up round them in the next century, relying mainly on the Greek texts and commentaries they had brought with them; translations were made from these and certain treatises from India into Persian or Syriac, and these were studied at the famous university, which the Abbasid Caliph Ma'mun founded at Bagdad in the 9th century, whence masters like Hunayn and al-Ibadi went out to collect scientific works and translate them into Arabic. From Bagdad knowledge spread along the Muslim roads as far as Spain, where scholars like Gerbert came to imbibe it.[1] After the fall of Cordoba, Toledo became the centre of translation; teams of Jews and Spaniards worked together under the inspiration of Archbishop Raimundo, and students gathered from

[1] Afterwards Pope Sylvester II. The knowledge he acquired at Cordoba so startled his contemporaries that he was credited with selling his soul to the Devil.

every part of Europe: Adelard of Bath, Robert of Chester, Michael the Scot, Hermann of Dalmatia and Hermann the German, Plato of Tivoli and so many others, who disseminated the new learning in their own countries.

．　　　．　　　．　　　．　　　．

East of the Mosque lay the Market, still easy to trace in a characteristic tight nexus of streets, many of them with names that still commemorate their ancient function: Alhondiga, the Corn Exchange: Alcaiceria, where drapers and mercers were grouped,[1] Cordoneros, Caldereros and Pescaderia—Haberdashers, Founders and Fishmongers. Much of the ancient market spilt across the Roman wall through the New Gate into the Ajerquia, which perpetuates the Arabic name of the Eastern Quarter; three streets in a row accommodated the Maltsters, the Skinners and the Saddlers, and still bear their names. There was another thriving shopping centre further north, round the gate where the Roman Via Augusta entered the old city: streets there are still named after butchers, shoemakers, booksellers and weavers of straw mats. The dealers in luxuries have not left their mark on the town map, though there is no doubt that the powerful aristocracy and the small but affluent *muwallad* middle class were keen buyers of the fine tissues woven in Almeria and Malaga, the silks of Valencia and Granada, the arms of Toledo and all those rich and rare products of foreign lands that enterprising Jews brought in through the port of Pechina. For carpets and leather-work their own city could not be bettered: but there is no trace at Cordoba as in most of the cities of the Levant of a "Bezesten", where all the goldsmiths and jewellers and dealers in ivories congregated: very probably because most of the finest work was carried on within the precincts of the palace, in dignified seclusion and security.

There also the most splendid tissues were woven under the eye of a royal officer called the *Sahib al-Tiraz*—the Master of Embroidery—whose function it was to furnish the robes of honour presented by the Sovereign to ambassadors or others whom he delighted to honour. His office was anything but a sinecure, calling for a professional knowledge of designs and processes, as well as the proper seasons for buying the requisite yarns and dyes. May was the time for the *qirmiz*, the cochineal

---

[1] The word has a respectable ancestry, going all the way back to the Caesars. It is the Arabic "al-Qaisariya", deriving from "Caesarea", an imperial market or town or port.

that yielded the prized crimson dye: August brought another
dye, the present-day *bleu Saxe*: September the madder with
another shade of red.   The silk yarn itself seems to have been
marketed in both May and August.   The designs were either
Sassanid or Coptic: the Umayyads favoured the former,
which was characterized by circles containing pairs of animal
figures balanced on either side of the Tree of Life, with their
heads turned back over their shoulders—an odd attitude which
is thought to derive from the Parthian habit of discharging
arrows while in flight. The African Almoravids and Almohads
preferred the Coptic designs, which affected bands and
polygonal *motifs*.

Some fragments of early tissues have survived: one famous
piece woven for Hisham was preserved as the lining of an ivory
casket at San Esteban de Gormaz: it is a mixture of silk and
wool with parallel bands on the Coptic model, showing polygonal ornaments and a Kufic inscription which allows it to be
dated with certainty.

A number of ivory caskets carved in the palace workshops
have also survived, mostly through being kept in church treasures: there is a wonderful cylindrical casket of al-Nasir's time
at Zamora: another rectangular one at Pamplona, which once
belonged to a son of Mansur: others at Palencia and Zaragoza
and the Louvre, and a very fine group in the Victoria and Albert
Museum.

.   .   .   .   .

The palace that accommodated these crafts in the time of
al-Nasir stood a few miles northeast of Cordoba: the present
approach takes you towards the monastery of San Jeronimo,
now the property of the Marques del Merito, whose private
landing-strip one crosses just before reaching the site.   Excava-
tion is proceeding slowly, as the government owns only a small
portion of the area, but enough of the principal halls has been
uncovered to prove that the rapturous descriptions of contemporary authors were not exaggerated.   Some of them
opening on to wide patios have been partially reconstructed:
the ground plan consists of five aisles, the inner three communi-
cating so intimately as to make a single apartment.   At the
head of the middle aisle, the Caliph's throne was set up, before
which obeisance had to be made, whether he occupied it or no.
Each of the outer aisles, which had access to the others by
narrower doors, contained at the upper end a smallish room
with a private bathroom and closet, the bath being a Roman

sarcophagus; these were assigned as sleeping quarters to visiting royalties, their suite being housed in the exterior aisle.

The whole area of the palace was equipped with an admirable system of drains, the sewers being high enough to allow a man to walk upright, though the manhole which gave access is so narrow that he would have to be lowered into it with his arms by his sides.

At a somewhat lower level, another great hall has been excavated and roofed over, and shows the carved stone revetments that covered the entire surface of the walls, which are still in place.[1]   A multitude of fragments of this dado are disposed on the floor and the surrounding area, in a vast jigsaw puzzle: two pieces of a beautiful rose-red stone stand out from the mass: no others like them have come to light; the riddle awaits its solution.

.   .   .   .   .

Madinat al-Zahra, as the name implies, was a city in itself: Abd al-Rahman III built it at the height of his power, an intelligent exercise in town-planning, housing the administration of the Empire and all the royal activities. His example has frequently been followed, in our own time at Canberra and New Delhi. The Arab historians however favour another explanation, which need not be quite untrue.   One of al-Nasir's concubines dying devised her fortune to the ransoming of Muslim captives in Christian hands; the Caliph's victories however had been so unbroken that the Christians had very few captives, and the ransoms paid made little impression on the legacy.   In doubt how to dispose of the remainder, the Caliph consulted another favourite, who suggested a new palace less cramped than the old Alcazar opposite the Great Mosque. The Caliph took her advice, gave the new palace her name, Madinat al-Zahra—City of the Flower, and set up her statue over the gate.   It is related that when the work was completed, the lady came to admire and was pained to see her statue framed in the dark mountain-side.   "Seest thou how the

---

[1] Lévi Provençal, most circumspect of *savants*, describes this as stucco: for once however he is at fault: it is stone, carefully worked and deeply carved; the only stucco is the occasional clumsy repairs made by one of the ephemeral Caliphs of the *fitna*. (The *fitna*, the troubles, was a convenient way of describing the years of anarchy that followed the death of Mansur's son Mudhaffar, when Cordoba was racked with the riots and revolutions in which the Caliphate dissolved into the fragmentary kingdoms known as the *Taifas*.)

beauty of the fair damsel is marred by the embrace of a negro?"
The omnipotent Caliph thought first of removing the mountain
to satisfy her, but eventually confined himself to replacing the
dark-leaved trees by figs and almonds.

The term "city" is by no means an exaggeration. The site
is all but a mile wide from east to west, and something less than
half a mile from north to south. It occupied three terraces,
each high enough above the next to allow a clear view; the
palace itself on the topmost, the middle all gardens and orchards,
while the lowest housed the offices in which the business of the
state was carried on, the residences of the great officers, barracks for the guard, a mint, armouries, hammams, workshops
and a mosque which some affirmed was lovelier than that of
Cordoba. The unexcavated ruins of its five aisles are plain to
see from the palace: its orientation is unexceptionable.

Al-Nasir tunnelled through the hills and built an aqueduct
which furnished an abundant supply of water, which now is
sadly lacking.

Architects from Constantinople and Bagdad supervised the
construction, which was pushed on at a great rate. Building
began in 936, and the sovereign was living there before 941,
when the mosque was dedicated. The Caliph continued to
lavish fortunes on embellishments till he died in 952, when his
son Hakam continued the work, but spent less on the palace
than the Cordoba mosque. A third of the revenues of Andalus
went to the building of al-Zahra; ten thousand workmen were
employed, fourteen hundred mules and four hundred camels
which belonged to the Caliph besides fifteen hundred pack-
animals hired at the rate of three *mithqals* a month. The workmen got less—from one and a half to two and a quarter
mithqals.

The chroniclers have described some of the apartments:
the Hall of the Caliphate with its doors of ebony and walls
sheathed in gold I have described elsewhere: another breath-
taking feature was the fountain which was brought from
Constantinople by Abd al-Rahman's Christian ambassador
Recemundo. It was set up in the Eastern Hall: there was a
basin of green marble in a frame of gilded bronze, with twelve
figures round it; on one side a lion between an antelope and a
crocodile; facing them a dragon and an eagle, and in between
a pigeon, a falcon, a duck, a hen, a cock, a kite and a vulture:
all of pure gold and wrought in Cordoba, and the water stream-
ing from their mouths. Nothing remains of them, but there is
a lovable little bronze stag in the Museum, to give an idea of

their beauty; it was found at Madinat al-Zahra, but belongs to another fountain.

The Flower City had a short life. Forty years' labour went to its making and adornment: forty years later it perished in the *fitna*. The Berbers forced an entrance in 1010, and after massacring the garrison and non-combatant residents, used the incomparable palace as their headquarters during the winter, and sacked it when they removed in the spring. Fourteen years later it was again pillaged by Mustakhfi: ibn Bassam writes contemptuously of this ephemeral ruler that it would be just such a weakling, with less strength than the muskrat and a feebler constitution than Nimrud's mosquito,[1] that Allah would select for such devastation: His are the power and the omnipotence. There was more systematic demolition twenty years later: "Allah gave strength to this little manikin like the vile rats that destroyed the dam at Marib": the columns and ornaments were sold to the highest bidder, and have been identified in many places. The *qibla* at Marrakesh, for example, has columns that bear Abd al-Rahman's name. Even so, the lakes and gardens retained a nostalgic charm, and al-Zahra was a favourite *rendez-vous* for poets and their mistresses. Ibn Zaydun reminds the princess Wallada of the happy hours they spent there together, rebuilding the palaces in fancy; and a young diplomat, who picnicked there in Mu'tamid's day, records how the park offered them vernal carpets embroidered with white flowers and bordered with runlets: the ruins of the palaces, like mothers deprived of their children, lamented their decay and the end of feasts, while lizards played among the stones, and crows cawed on the crumbling walls.

For succeeding centuries the ruins were a quarry for all and sundry: the monastery of San Jeronimo was built from them; the end came when the present bull-breeding establishment built all the miles of walls that enclose the paddocks. "Blessed be He that brings down marvels, and alters the face of countries."

---

[1] Who chastened that monarch for his pride by entering his brain through his nostril and giving him a perpetual migraine.

CHAPTER THREE

THE PEOPLE

Too much has been made of the predominance of Arab blood in Andalusia: it is still the practice of irate Spaniards from other parts to call the Andalusians "*Moros*" and point to the swarthy colouring of some of them. While sympathizing with them in their ineffectual exasperation, cooler observers will remember that they have encountered a similar prevalence of dark pigmentation in many other parts of Spain, and incline to attribute the traits that annoy the northerner more to climate than Arab descent. But there is undoubtedly something in it: you have only to spend successive weeks in Catalonia and Andalusia to come part of the way round to their view.

Before the Muslim Conquest the basic Celto-Iberian stock had taken up a slight tincture of Greco-Phoenician blood and a heavier Gothic and Roman admixture, the last incorporating strains from whatever barbarians made up the fighting strength of the occupying armies, since the Romans themselves had given up fighting. The population also included a sizable Jewish minority, probably more inbred than the rest, by reason on the one hand of Jewish aloofness and on the other of the Gentiles' unwillingness to mate with them.

The Muslim conquerors, when they came, were no overwhelming hordes but a singularly scanty force composed of Syrians and Berbers; as soon as the first Abd al-Rahman was fairly established, these were reinforced by members of the Umayyad family and their freedmen from the East, and by frequent new accessions of Berbers, either immigrants or mercenaries imported by the Amirs. This "Moorish" preponderance was deliberately weakened by the ruling family, who called in the Slavonians as a counterpoise to the Arab party's ambitions: these comprised not only the first lot of European slaves brought in by Jewish traders, who were in fact Slavs, but eventually all white-complexioned slaves from any part of Europe, and all the adventurers who came to seek fortune under the Caliphal banners.

Another factor whose importance tends to be overlooked is the unwavering predilection of the conquerors for Spanish women, and the latter's marked capacity for assimilating foreign strains. This is exemplified in present-day Malaga, where most of the prominent families have one or more foreign grandparents, but foreign traits are rarely perceptible. Under the Caliphate this prepotency of the Spanish element had been at work for a century and a half, so that at the opening of the 10th century the great al-Nasir belonged to the seventh generation born in Andalus, his sole pure-blooded Syrian ancestor being Abd al-Rahman I. All his forefathers in the direct line had taken Spanish wives, so that quantitatively the proportion of Arab blood in his veins was less than one in a hundred. In quality however it may reasonably be argued that that small trace exerted a powerful stimulus on the rest, to produce certain exceptional characteristics.

The people over whom the Caliph ruled were far from forming a homogeneous compound, but when he ascended the throne there were already some signs of a growing Andalusian consciousness, not yet advanced enough to be called national, but making progress in that direction during his long and victorious reign. There were still many sharp divisions of race and creed and caste, and bitter antipathies that obstructed the development of a corporate sense. For one thing, the Arabs had brought with them to Spain all their ancient tribal feuds, and nursed them assiduously; in the first years of the Conquest they had plagued the administration with their incessant private wars, until a strong Governor had resettled the petulant tribes in country as nearly as possible like their native abiding places and removed as far as possible from their dearest enemies. Even so their hereditary quarrels still persisted in the Caliph's time, and it was not till a century later that they finally faded out, when Mansur reorganized the army, breaking up the traditional tribal contingents into regiments formed on a regional basis. Then at last the tribal *nisbas*—clan names—which had kept their vendettas alive were replaced by new names, mostly territorial and taken from their Spanish homes.

Meantime the Arabs behaved as a privileged aristocracy, residing in the capitals on the income from their estates in the rich valleys, which they had acquired as first-comers, arrogating to themselves a monopoly of lucrative posts in the government, but sedulously avoiding anything that smacked of plebeian hard work.

The Berbers were mostly dispersed over the less fertile hill-country, where they carried on subsistence farming in conditions similar to those of their native mountains. They were

loathed and despised by the Arabs: Pérès quotes an epigram
by an anonymous poet that summarizes this attitude:

> I dreamt of Adam; "Father of men," I said,
> "They say that the Berber tribe is descended from Thee."
> He replied, "I repudiate Eve, if they speak truth."

The aversion was so deeply rooted as to be universally taken for
granted: when the youthful Mu'tamid sustained a regrettable
defeat at Malaga, he could risk telling his redoubtable father
that it was all the fault of the Berbers, though history assigns
much of the responsibility to certain singing-girls. A more
professional soldier, Musa ibn Nusayr, who directed the Conquest, put on record his profound distaste for their malignance
and treachery, while getting the best out of their fighting qualities. The geographers explained their notorious shortcomings
by the fact that they lived in the Third Climate, which everyone
agreed was inhabited by men disposed to jealousy, rancour
and malevolence, and deriving pleasure from the shedding of
human blood. Qalqashandi embroiders a little: "Although
the Third Climate, according to those that dwell in it, is subject
to the influence of Mercury, it possesses the above characters,
especially in the farther west: the inhabitants glory in murder,
and strangle a man as they would a sparrow." And ibn Abdun
recommends special precautions against their predacious habits.

Nevertheless they occasionally threw up a distinguished
doctor of law, like the famous Mundhir ibn Sa'id al Balluti and
Yahya ibn Yahya: and there is no doubt that they were bonny
fighters. On the collapse of the Caliphate certain Berber
families set up *taifas* in Andalus, and the two dynasties, Almoravid and Almohad, that took the country from the *taifa* kings,
gave evidence of remarkable talent in war, though the fleshpots of Andalus soon sapped their energies; and it was a Berber
dynasty, the Ziris, that held out at Granada till the end.

The natives who formed the great bulk of the population
(leaving the Jews on one side) fall into two categories, the
larger consisting of those Christians who embraced Islam
either at the Conquest or later, and the smaller those that
remained faithful to their religion. The former were classified
under further sub-heads by the conquerors, according to the
circumstances of their conversion, which made all the difference
to their wealth and standing. Those leading Goth families
that made common cause with the invaders were accepted on
terms of equality, kept all their property and were able to maintain an almost royal state: two hundred years later we find

The Portillo at Cordoba

A street in Carmona

Puerta del Sol at Toledo

a historian complacently referring to his descent from Sara the Goth. Others, who accepted Islam only after defeat, naturally received less favourable treatment, though they also benefited from the enlightened tolerance of the Umayyad Amirs, who adopted them as their *mawlas*. In a comparatively short time they all came to be lumped together under the name of *muwallad* (the Spanish *muladi*), a term which originally meant the child of a Muslim father or mother, but eventually covered every kind of apostate or his descendants. These *muwallads*, with those who remained Christian, constituted the majority of the population, and almost the whole of the productive classes: craftsmen and small tradesmen in the towns, farmers and labourers in the countryside.

Many of these conversions to Islam were spurious, inspired exclusively by the desire for the privileges of a Muslim: the Christians and Jews who refused to change their faith were treated as *dhimmis*, a subject class, and had to pay the *jizya*, a poll-tax from which professing Muslims were exempt. They suffered other disabilities, including the risk of fanatical mob violence, which was however rarer than might have been expected. The genuine Muslims probably felt more respect for the Christian who stuck to his faith than for the *muwallad*, whose sincerity was not so certain.

The Christians, who besides their *bourgeois* avocations in the towns had whole villages to themselves in country districts like the Serrania, were known as mozarabes,[1] an odd name derived from the Arabic *musta'rib*, which by its grammatical form would signify a man who wished to pass for an Arab, an aper of Arab fashions; an example of *lucus a non lucendo*, one would think, as the Mozarabes had chosen to keep their own customs. They justified their name however to a certain extent, in the sense that they were prompt to adopt the Arabic language: an angry Bishop berates them for their indifference to good Latin, as he cannot staff his churches; and in the larger cities like Cordoba, Seville and Zaragoza, where they lived cheek by jowl with the Muslims, they dressed like them. Their preference for Arabic is illustrated by the custom of the Mozarabes in Toledo of writing Spanish in Arabic characters a century after Alfonso VI captured the town.[2]

[1] This was perhaps the term they used themselves: the Arabs called them "*ajam*" or "*ajami*", a word now current in the Levant with the contemptuous sense of stupid or inexpert.

[2] The Spanish Jews who used to make up the great majority of the population of Salonica still spoke Spanish four and a half centuries after their ancestors were expelled, but wrote it in Hebrew characters.

D

They were as a rule on the best of terms with their renegade brethren, serving not infrequently under the same banner: it was this fusion of *muwallad* and *mozarabe* that enabled Umar ibn Hafsun to hold out so long.   As for their loyalty to the Amir, it is clear that although they were prepared to follow a rebel chieftain in a purely domestic revolt, they did not in general respond to the appeals that came from the other side of the frontier, until the intolerance of the Almoravids drove them to despair.   Only then did the incursions of the Christian kings meet with assistance from the *mozarabes* on their paths: otherwise how could Alfonso VI have maintained his four thousand horsemen for nine months in enemy country?   But the reckoning proved how wise their earlier caution had been.   When Alfonso withdrew from Andalusia, thousands of *mozarabes* followed him for fear of reprisals; from those that remained Ali ibn Yusuf expelled whole communities to North Africa, settling the towns of Safi and Meknes with them, and creating a bodyguard for himself of desperate and homeless Christians who could be counted on to defend him against the Maghribis.

The Almohads went even further in intolerance: in 1147 Abd al-Mu'min said his rule admitted only of Muslims, and ordered churches and synagogues to be razed; and when he took Seville a few months later, the Christian bishops who had till then enjoyed a sort of extraterritorial immunity, hastily packed up and made for Toledo.

Of all the elements that went to the make-up of the Spaniard, few have as fascinating a history as the Jews.   From Roman times there was a large Jewish minority, possibly transplanted from Jerusalem by Hadrian (himself an Andalusian) when he finally crushed the rebellion of Barcochebas.   When Rome went down, the Goths made persistent efforts to convert them to Christianity: successive Councils of Toledo round the end of the 6th century passed or revived decrees imposing baptism in mixed marriages under pain of exile: between 612 and 620, according to Murphy, ninety thousand Jews were forcibly baptized, a convocation being set up to see that the new Christians attended all the offices.   The *Fuero Juzgo* of the 7th century forbade the celebration of the Passover or circumcision or marriage according to Jewish rite, and laid down that any Jew who failed to give his child Christian baptism should receive a hundred lashes, forfeit his land to the king and have his head shaven for a sign.   In 681 at the twelfth Council of Toledo King Euric issued a veritable corpus of laws, that was equivalent to complete proscription: Jews had to become Christian

within the year or leave the country. It was impossible to
enforce compliance, so the Goths fell back on the easier and
more profitable policy of fines and disabilities, till in 694
another Council ordered them to be sold into slavery, except for
their children under seven years of age, who were to be brought
up as Christians.   It is not surprising that the Jews extended an
enthusiastic welcome to the Moorish invaders, and undertook
with delight the duty of holding the cities down behind them.

They met with the accustomed careless tolerance of the
Muslim: once they had paid their poll-tax, they were free to
engage in trade or other occupation, and their native genius
and enterprise soon won them a strong position in the economy
of the country.   They had their own quarters in every town
of any importance: in Cordoba a large section near the Alcazar
still bears their name: in Toledo they lived in a separate
madina, surrounded by a strong wall: in certain towns, such as
Tarragona, Granada and Lucena, they eventually acquired a
complete ascendancy.   From an early date the last was their
great headquarters, the richest Jews residing within a moat and
strong wall, where Muslims were not allowed to enter.

Granada always had a large Jewish population: by the 10th
century it was known as the City of the Jews.   The last Ziri
king, whose memoirs written in 1090 have been translated by
Lévi-Provençal, says that in the time of his father Badis most of
the inhabitants were Jews, and the king had two Jewish prime
ministers in succession.   The first was a man of remarkable
talent, respected and admired by the Muslims, but his son, who
succeeded him, had far less *doigté* and so incensed the Muslims
as to provoke a pogrom.

The history of the Jews in Andalus interested fewer
chroniclers than their history under the Christians.   It is
pretty certain that a high percentage of the trade of the
country was in their hands, and in particular they gave evidence
of a highly venturesome disposition in voyaging to the ends of
the earth in search of profit.   Their mastery of languages and
their international organization gave them a big advantage
over competitors, but it needed a stout heart to set sail for Egypt
or Syria in the cranky ships of those days,[1] with the constant
menace of pirates, and to cross Arabia or Iraq to Sind and

[1] The poets regarded sea voyages with horror and never embarked
without grave misgivings.   Pérès records the protest of one of them, whose
patron called on him to take ship.   "Heaven crown you with blessings,"
he writes, "but keep this injunction for someone else.   You are not Noah
to save me in the Ark: I am not Moses to walk the waves."

China in search of those perfumes and spices, gems and rare tissues, which returned the highest dividends. They were foredoomed by their financial genius to incur the hatred of their fellow-citizens, for no-one but themselves was capable of organizing the collection of taxes, though in matters of simple usury the Christians easily held their own.[1]

They excelled in medicine and diplomacy: the famous Hasday ibn Shaprut was both physician and ambassador to al-Nasir. Their skill in science made them obnoxious to the Muslim *faqihs*: ibn Abdun says sourly that they should not be allowed to doctor any but their own people: why trust them with Muslim lives, for which they have no affection? Moreover they should be forbidden to buy Arabic books of learning: the Christians no less: they all translate them and pretend that their bishops and rabbis wrote them. The Christian councils also ordained that they should not physic Christians nor employ Christian nurses nor occupy posts of honour near kings and other secular authorities; and Christian evidence should prevail against Jewish, if indeed they were heard in evidence at all.

In Muslim Spain they fitted better into the background and enjoyed a greater measure of tolerance: consequently they could devote themselves with greater serenity to study, and so threw up a number of distinguished philosophers, such as Maimonides of Cordoba and Abraham ben Ezra of Tudela (Browning's Ben Ezra) in the 12th century, and Avicebron (Salomon ibn Gabirol) of Malaga in the 11th: politicians like Shemuel ibn Negrela, *wazir* of Granada and Abu 'l-Fadl ibn Hasday, *wazir* of Zaragoza, in the 11th century: and poets like ibn Sahl, a *converso* of Seville, perhaps the inventor of the *zajal* in the 13th.

On the Christian side of the frontier they were less fortunate: they could not escape the unpopular (but not unremunerative) task of fleecing the poor for the benefit of the powerful: the consequent loathing of the common people for them is enshrined in the Cantar de Mio Cid, which relates with gusto how the Cid gets money out of the Jews Raquel and Vidas, by depositing with them a chest which he swears contains gold, but is in fact full of sand. This chest or a successor is still shown with equal gusto in Burgos cathedral.

[1] S. W. Baron in his "Social and Religious History of the Jews" remarks that in the Middle Ages the interest they charged varied between thirty-three per cent and forty-five per cent; but after the Jews were expelled from Naples Christian rates went up to two hundred and forty per cent.

The Kings however and the nobles found the Jews a convenient source of income and protected them while they amassed the wealth on which they intended to draw. In the 14th century we find Alfonso XI pressing Pope Clement VI to let the Jews meet at a new synagogue, on the ground that their contribution to the needs of the town was absolutely necessary. He encourages the Pope to permit this infraction of the rule, by asserting that they fought against the Saracens side by side with the Christians. The Church also had an eye on that accumulated wealth, but regarded it not as a banking account on which to draw but as a treasure to be looted at a stroke.[1] They had an additional motive for disapproving of the Jews: not only were they enemies of the Faith, but also efficient collectors of revenue. It is regrettable to relate that certain ecclesiastics were so constantly suspected of cheating over their tithes that Juan I was obliged to forbid them to begin weighing their corn on the threshing-floor until the church bells had rung to summon the *terceros*, who collected the king's third.

On all sides then the Jews bred ill will, the hatred which the people felt for them, the colder malevolence of the Church, and finally the festering bitterness between Church and King on their account, which gave birth to the Inquisition, when at last the Dominicans achieved the ascendancy for which they had been fighting for two centuries and more. There was a great difference between the positions of one Fernando at the beginning of the 14th century and another more famous at the end of the 15th. In 1307 the canons of Toledo had obtained a bull from Pope Clement V, instructing them not only not to discharge their debts to the Jews but also to recover the interest they had paid. The Jews appealed to their natural protector Fernando IV, who curtly ordered the canons to desist from persecuting "his" Jews. In 1481 Fernando el Catolico had a similar brush with the Archbishop of Zaragoza: he wrote a letter on the same lines, but found no-one who dared deliver it.

Hated as they were by Church and *pueblo llano*, the Jews still identified themselves with their country and contributed in many ways to its evolution and expansion. The nobles did not share the abhorrence of Jewry: intermarriage was constant, with less prejudice on the Spanish than the Jewish side. Many of the proudest families took Jewish wives, attracted by their wealth, intelligence and good looks: before the 15th century such alliances scandalized no-one. Jewish blood flowed even

[1] The Summa Theologia lays it down that since the Jews are the slaves of the Church, the Church can dispose of their goods.

in royal veins: for the Admiral don Alonso Enriquez, who descended on one side from Alonso XI and Enrique el Viejo and on the other from a Jewish banker (and had no inhibitions about it), had a daughter who married Juan II of Aragon and was the mother of Fernando el Catolico himself. Most noble families had a Jew in their family tree: Francisco Mendoza y Bobadilla, Cardinal Archbishop of Burgos, took the trouble to write a treatise proving that not only his own noble parents had Jewish blood, but there were very few aristocrats who had none.

The Jews inclined to be more scrupulous on the point: in the 12th and 13th centuries they were issuing certificates of pure Jewish descent, uncontaminated by Gentile taint; and Salomon Halevi, chief rabbi in Burgos, wrote a discourse on the Origin and Nobility of his Lineage, in which he vaunted his unsullied Jewish descent. It is depressing to record that at a later date, when he had been converted to Christianity and enthroned as Bishop of Burgos, he was a sturdy advocate of pogroms.

He was not the only Bishop of Burgos of Jewish extraction. In the following century another *converso*, Alonso of Cartagena, who occupied the archiepiscopal throne, was despatched to the Council of Basle as envoy of Castille, to defend her claim to precedence of England. His argument—which carried the day—included *en passant* an appreciation of Cosimo dei Medici, which must have ruffled that magnate's feathers, asking (with no doubt about the answer) whether it was remotely possible that a tradesman, however wealthy, should take precedence of a Spanish duke. This *morgue* was not peculiar to the Jews who lived in the Christian kingdoms: we find it also in Muslim Spain: the scholar Avicebron is just as caustic about the Christians. "How can one live among people who cannot distinguish their right hand from their left? . . . Their ancestors were not fit to serve as dogs to my people's flocks: they fancy themselves giants, but to me look like locusts."

But by and large they served the Christian rulers with loyalty and distinction, and the three great Spanish Orders of Chivalry were all glad to profit by their skill. The association of one Rabbi Moshe Arragel with the Military Order of Cala-trava produced one of the loveliest books in the world. The Grand Master, don Luis de Guzman, set Rabbi Moshe to translate the Bible into the Romance tongue, with notes and illustrations (*glosada e ystoriada*); he spent eight years on the work, which was engrossed and illuminated magnificently, and presented to don Luis in 1430, who thus achieved his life's ambition of reading the Scriptures in his own tongue. This is the famous Bible of the House of Alba, which was given in 1624 by the Grand Inquisitor to the 5th Duke of Alba, in recognition of his father's labours *pro fide* in the Dutch Wars.

In much the same way Gomez Suarez de Figueroa, the son of the Master of the Order of Santiago, commissioned the translation of Maimonides' principal work, the More Nebuchim, or Instruction of the Perplexed.

The Spanish Orders of Chivalry never acquired the commercial and financial attainments of the Templars, and were hardly ever capable of looking after their own interests; so they employed Jewish contractors. In 1272 the Master of the Order of Santiago farmed out to don Bondon Jacobo and don Samuel the collection of the rents of all the Order's properties in Murcia, Toledo, la Mancha and Granada. Their work was satisfactory, for he renewed the lease in 1273 and 1274. A few years later all the Order's properties in Carmona were leased to a Jew, in payment of a debt: a special clause was written into the deed that he must repair the mill, using good mortar, and restore it to its condition when the Moors had it a generation or so before.

The most enlightened instance of this association of the Orders of Chivalry with Jews is furnished by don Juan de Zuñiga, the last Grand Master of the Order of Alcántara. At the University of Salamanca he followed the courses of Antonio de Nebrija (who introduced the study of Latin into Spain), and carried off the professor to his palace near Cáceres. There he set up an Academy under the direction of the great astronomer, Abraham Zacuto, who read the spheres for him and painted an astronomical map in an upper chamber. He also wrote a book on the influences of the heavens, for the instruction of the physicians of the Order.

Abraham Zacuto exerted a profound if indirect influence on the course of world history: after Fernando el Catolico had persuaded don Juan de Zuñiga to hand over to him the Office of Grand Master and the revenues of the Order—this was in 1494 or 1495—Abraham was in Portugal, and supplied the explorer Vasco da Gama with his nautical instruments and a perpetual almanac of his devising. His pupil Joseph Vecinho, a servant of King John II of Portugal and a geographer in his own right, was one of the committee of five appointed by that monarch to examine the plans of Christopher Columbus: the others were the Bishop of Ceuta, a German cartographer named Martin Behaim, a court physician, and a mathematician named Moses. Of these five the last certainly was a Jew, the physician probably and the German possibly. In addition Columbus received financial support from Isaac Abravanel, another Jew and John's Minister of Finance, who also wrote a commentary on the Bible. The extent of Jewish participation in the venture is astonishing: there were at least five Jewish interpreters on the strength, and within three weeks of Columbus's first landfall, one of the two men he sent out on an important reconnaissance was a Jew named Luis de Torres. I have wondered whether he was the first European to experiment with tobacco, but history is silent on this subject.

.   .   .   .   .

All these diverse people got along very well in ordinary times, living very much the same life, for all their fundamental differences in origin and creed, dressing alike, when the government let them, talking the same vernacular, celebrating one another's feasts with an eclectic gusto, and in their friendships and their quarrels following personal rather than racial or religious *penchants*; a compound, in the chemical sense, rather than a mixture, that tended towards a civic, even a national outlook. The lines of cleavage were there, and show up under stress: but in normal circumstances if the Slavonians were disliked, it is not because they were Slavonians but because they had perquisites that the others lacked. The Arab aristocracy was unpopular, not because they belonged to a different race, but because at the Conquest they had seized and still held the richest land in the country, and had built themselves lordly mansions in the city. The Berbers were different: they were uneasy neighbours; there were too many of them for one thing, so many that the Great Mosque at Cordoba had to be enlarged over and over again. This anti-Berber feeling became a sort of catalyst that set off the fusion of the rest into an Andalusian people; and the savageries of the *fitna* show how deep this cleavage goes.

Perhaps even more efficient in transmuting the various elements into a people was the fact that all of them had taken wives in the country, and had been unobtrusively moulded by the powerful influence of the Spanish women: retiring, meek, submissive, yielding, but always triumphant.

.   .   .   .   .

The towns these people lived in, like most towns of the Middle Ages, were completely unplanned: irregular clots of buildings separated by tortuous narrow streets, sometimes cobbled, more often just the beaten earth, but rarely lacking the kennel down the middle which served for drainage. The frontage of the houses occupied by Muslims was blank and windowless, and where the Christians lived in the same quarter, they would build on the same plan. The lowlier houses had walls of adobe bricks or *pisé*; the roof was made of branches interlaced and plastered with clay and rendered to some extent waterproof by a compost of lime, ashes and the lees of olive oil: not very staunch, but good enough for a country where rain was rare and life was preordained. Here and there a larger house, with two stories, belonging to a successful Jew perhaps, and sometimes the mansion of a grandee, standing in its own grounds, like that palace of ibn Futais's that occupied a whole quarter at Cordoba: here he kept his incomparable library in a great building decorated throughout in green, for the protection of the manuscripts and the comfort of the six copyists that he kept permanently occupied, paying them not according to the number of folios they turned out, but the time they spent on them, lest they be tempted to hurry by the lure of piece-work.

The ground-plan of these cities was based on the roads that led from one of the principal gates to another: smaller lanes grew out of these without system or design, much as mould develops on the glass slip of a scientist: at the intersection of the chief roads an open space, affording a breath of fresh air after the stinking alleys, where the residents could congregate for any social purpose, a market or a show; later, in Christian times, this was to be expanded into an ambitious Plaza Mayor, on a more or less symmetrical plan, to form a lordly promenade for townsfolk and visitors, which could be quickly converted into a bull-ring by blocking the issues.

The house-plan was the same as in present-day Muslim cities: an unobtrusive door gave access to a passage *en chicane* to protect the womenfolk from curious eyes: this led to an open space or patio with rooms strung round it. This patio would be as rectangular as the shape of the ground allowed, and there might be a partial upper floor with a gallery overlooking it. In the houses of the wealthy there would be an inner court for the women-folk: the master of the house attended to business and received visitors in the outer patio: both courts might have a fountain in the middle and orange- and lemon-trees in beds that ran parallel to the sides. Such mansions had frequently efficient drainage systems, though the outflow would probably not be carried further than the street outside. Even this contrivance was well in advance of European practice for many centuries later: latrines with water drainage were not infrequent in quite lowly establishments. When the Alcazabilla of Malaga was cleared of its slums, a group of miniature houses was uncovered, each supplied with a closet discreetly tucked away at the end of a passage, with a water conduit below. Excavations in Samarra revealed similar feats of plumbing in houses of the 9th century.

The most important buildings after the Alcazar were the mosques. These, like Christian churches, were places of assembly, not only for worship but for any respectable purpose. Their courtyards provided the only open spaces beside the central market for such as desired to take the air without resorting to the cemeteries outside the walls. They were the clubs of the age, where honest men met and passed the time of day and kept abreast of events: the principal mosque was the natural centre to which travellers would repair on arrival, and where distinguished *savants* could give a course of lectures. The qadi sat in judgment in his favourite corner and dealt out summary and equitable decisions. Towards evening both mosque and courtyard would be thronged with gregarious citizens, and the street vendors would flock to this opportune market to hawk their wares: a practice which ibn Abdun viewed with disfavour but had no hope of preventing. In Egypt, never noted for elegant manners, the tone was far less refined: ibn Hawkal was shocked to see parties picnicking inside the mosque, and al-Muqaddasi was horrified to see Egyptians hawking and spitting and cleaning their noses, and hiding the unspeakable under the carpets.

No such grossness, of course, in the mosques of Muslim Spain: the Andalusian had his faults, but they were not of this brutish nature. Indeed ibn Bashkuwal gave Cordoba society a singularly good character; commending the solidity of their faith, the honest foundation of their wealth, the neatness of their clothing, the smart turn-out of their horses, and the elevation of their sentiments. The great rival Seville also had its champions: the population was a thought less Victorian, but far more cheerful and enterprising: if you asked for birds' milk in Seville, it would be found. And then what a town! A river above all other rivers, says al-Shaqundi, because it is bordered with villas, gardens, vineyards and poplars without a break: "one I knew who had been in Egypt said that the Nile was not so: and another who knew Bagdad said he preferred Seville because good spirits are never wanting, for there is no

prohibition of music or wine, so long as drunkenness does not
give rise to quarrels".

There was inevitably another side to all this distinction and
bonhomie: Maqqari tells us that although there was a watchman
in every street to look after the gate that sealed it off at night,
and he had arms and a lamp and a dog, "nevertheless the
Andalusians are so cunning and skilled in contrivances that
they scale high buildings and open intricate bolts, and kill the
owner of the goods they steal in case he should denounce
them. Rarely passes a day without news of So-and-So having his throat cut." This is why ibn Abdun insists on the
zalmedina being an Andalusian, not an Almoravid, partly
of course because it would be awkward for an Almoravid
prince to ask one of his own people to submit his accounts
for scrutiny, but chiefly because it takes an Andaluz to be
up sides with his compatriots. Not excepting his own per-
sonnel: he must never omit to check his Dogberrys' reports
by written statements by the neighbours, "because they
prefer evil to good, since they get their food and clothing by
it, and the more there are of them, the worse mischief they get
into".

There were of course public baths—hammams—which
enjoyed a tremendous vogue among the Muslims. Not however a Muslim invention: the Arabs called them *hammam al-
Rumi*—Roman baths—and if the Romans did not invent them,
they undoubtedly brought them to perfection. They were
regarded with suspicion by the more devout, one of the chief
causes of offence being the statues and mosaics that were still
used for decoration. There are several references to repre-
sentations of the *'anqa* or phoenix, which Mez identifies with
the cherubim of the Ancient East, a bird with a human face and
legs, with four wings each side and clawed hands, differing only
from the Hebrew Seraph by possessing an additional set of
wings. The Spanish Muslims had no prejudice against repre-
sentation of human or animal forms, though the *faqihs* constantly inveighed against the practice: their baths were
frequently adorned with statues and pictures, many of them of
a decidedly indelicate character. Statues seem to have played
havoc with Muslim emotions. In one of the baths at Seville
there was a statue described by several authors which had been
brought from Italica, the Roman capital of Andalus and the
birthplace of three emperors. It portrayed a woman seated
with a child on her lap, so lovely and so captivating that a
number of the inhabitants went mad with hopeless love. The

subject of the group is obscure; it included a snake, which may have been just the *genius loci*.

The baths were built on the traditional plan that survives in the Near East: a vestibule for undressing, and a series of rooms each hotter than the last, and finally a cooler room, where swathed in towels the bather spent an hour readjusting himself to the outside temperature. They were immensely popular, many *habitués* taking pleasure in the convention that when both are naked Jack is as good as his master. (In Turkey to-day the attendant addresses one in the second person singular, which would be discourteous outside.) One poet however is quoted by Pérès as cursing them for just that reason; that savant and boor were equal and good manners lacking. The strictures of the pious were directed against hammams also as haunts of sodomy, and there is plenty of evidence that that reputation was merited.

In the afternoons the baths passed into feminine hands, the entire staff changing over, with the exception of the porter at the entrance. The women took possession for long hours of recreation and gossip, bringing their slaves and make-up specialists: doubtless a towel was hung over the entrance, as now, to warn the absentminded of the change of occupancy.

There were a surprising number of baths in the capitals. During the reign of the Caliph al-Nasir one traveller records three hundred at Cordoba: under Mansur another counts six hundred; in a town of half a million inhabitants this would perhaps not be excessive. When the Christians were installed as conquerors, far fewer baths satisfied their needs. The Moors had left very few villages without one, and when the Christians took over, they laid down precise regulations for the management of these questionable concerns. The 13th century *fuero* or statute of Zorita, a village in the Guadalajara, provides that men shall frequent them on Tuesday, Thursday and Saturday, women on Monday and Wednesday, Jews on Friday and Sunday. "And let no-one, man or woman, pay for entry more than one obol. And if anyone takes anything away, let them cut his ear off." [1]

In general the Christian Church viewed with horror this indulgence of the flesh and discountenanced the use of the bath

[1] "Viri eant ad communem balneum in die Martis et in die Jovis et in die sabbati: mulieres eant in die lune et in die Mercuri: Iudei eant in die Veneris et in die Dominica. Et nemo det sive mulier sive vir pro introitu balnei nisi obolum tantum." Amerigo Castro: España en la Historia.

by Christians; by the 16th century they were trying to prevent even Muslims from bathing. In 1567 they had their way: after a long and solemn ceremony all the baths at Granada were ritually put out of commission, *ad majorem Del gloriam*.

. . . . . .

Though the Andalusians were proud of their cities, their heart was really in the country—rather a formalized country, to be sure, nicely brushed and combed, with neat houses standing in pleasant gardens; their outlook was curiously like that of the Edwardian week-ender. Their poets boasted of the towns and the palaces within their precincts, (not a word about Cordoba's great mosque and the bridge across the Guadalquivir), but nothing gave them more intimate satisfaction than to escape to the surrounding fields. All who had the means built themselves *munyas*, country houses: the first Umayyad ruler set the fashion with his *munya* named nostalgically Rusafa after his ancestral pleasance in Syria: another built one called Dimishq; but these were modest structures, completely eclipsed by the magnificent palaces of al-Zahra and al-Zahira, built by al-Nasir and Mansur. But everyone who could built himself a little cottage, which he whitewashed diligently inside and out, as is still the custom, and all these hamlets sparkling among the trees "like pearls in a setting of emeralds" produced an atmosphere of comfort and prosperity, which must have been hard to find elsewhere. Seville had its own sylvan setting in the hills whose Arabic name still survives—Aljarafe—clothed in olive-gardens and orchards: al-Shaqundi describes the villages so tenderly cared for, looking like stars in an olive sky. "One who knew Cairo and Damascus," he says, "told me that the Aljarafe is a forest without lions and its river a Nile without crocodiles."

The other towns found their panegyrists, the poets being happiest with those that stand in fertile country, like Valencia and Granada and Berja with their rich *vegas* crisscrossed by springs and watercourses. In such surroundings the Andalusian preferred to live, either permanently or at least occasionally: those families whose modest means did not allow them to purchase the cottage of their dreams, would lose no chance of a picnic or a *romeria*, kept up perhaps under the blossomed trees throughout the warm and lucent night, returning in the early morning to their home in the mean street, when the husband would take up the basket and go off to the market, his wife settle down to the daily task of kneading the dough or washing the scanty linen, while the children took the pitchers and went to fetch the water: all facing the household routine with renewed courage after the refreshment of the country air, and doubtless congratulating themselves on their good fortune in living in their matchless city.

CHAPTER FOUR

ADMINISTRATION

AT A time like the present, when honest men are harassed by a monstrous brood of officials, it is a relief to turn to the Caliphate of Cordoba, a society governed by one competent and visible autocrat instead of thousands of petty jacks-in-office lurking in the dark anonymity of boards and departments, with no souls to lose and no body to kick. It is however consoling to see an increasing perception that that universal suffrage which was so long and so confidently proclaimed a panacea for all human disorder is workable only in a community so small that every member is personally familiar with the officers to whom he entrusts the administration.

The Greek inventors of democracy saw its dangers and provided the appropriate safety-valve: whenever a city state had outgrown manageable proportions, the excess was spawned off, the redundant members being ceremoniously but firmly sent off to found a new colony, that would be small enough to satisfy that essential condition of democracy; for the Greeks' acute political sense apprehended that an unwieldy community was the dedicated victim of politicians and the slave of its elected servants.

These perils indeed were not wanting in Cordoba, which was as liable to error as any other human assembly; and there were many occasions, particularly in its decline, when agitators took advantage of mob emotions, or a pretorian order conspired to rule. Such diseases of the body politic called for surgical treatment, and this was not seldom applied by a master hand: Cordoba never flourished more than when the sovereign wielded undisputed power, and had no scruples about using it.

In the early days of Islam the ruler dealt personally with every problem that presented itself, decided on policy towards neighbouring communities, led his people into battle when other means of persuasion failed, sat under a tree to hear and resolve the complaints or aspirations of his subjects, administering justice directly and without delay. Those were the patriarchal days when any Muslim had direct access to the Caliph: according to a sound *hadith* this is one of the four obligations which Umar ibn al-Khattab laid down for his successors—not to ride a horse nor wear fine linen nor eat

sweets nor set a doorkeeper to deny entrance to those in
need.

The Umayyad rulers in Damascus had a natural propensity
to simplicity and informality: nothing pleased them more than
to escape to the desert and resume the free and easy life of the
bedouin; and when Abd al-Rahman, the last survivor,
established Umayyad dominion in Spain, he introduced their
somewhat bohemian ways and allowed great freedom of access
to the sovereign. But as his dominions expanded and the
population multiplied, the increasing volume and complexity
of public business made it physically impossible for him to give
everything his personal attention, and he was obliged to dele-
gate the conduct of much of it to lieutenants: but though the
authority of those high functionaries was undisputed, it was in
no sense independent, and lasted no longer than the sovereign's
good pleasure. He could dismiss them as he could appoint
them, without explanation or justification; he remained the
absolute master: they were only extensions of his personality
and nothing at all without his consent.

In course of time, however, these officers commanded an
extensive network of subordinates, whose duty was to carry out
the policy laid down by the Sultan and report to them on
matters that called or might call for their attention. This civil
service acquired a quasi-permanency denied to the ministers
who directed it, (a phenomenon familiar in Whitehall to-day),
and like civil services in other times and places evolved its
peculiar jargon and punctilio about forms of address and similar
grave matters. To-day an ambassador might raise his eyebrows if the Secretary of State omitted to assure him that with
great truth and respect he was his obedient servant: so in
Cordoba a provincial engineer would expect his "God protect
and pardon you", while the really great, like the general commanding in Syria, would be roused to anger by anything less
than "God strengthen you, keep your life and grant you all his
kindness and beneficence". These things have their importance, particularly to those that have climbed ladders.[1]

Civil servants were no more popular then than to-day, and
for much the same reasons. A 9th century poet called them
"bilious hucksters who fill their paunches while the people

[1] The Christians inherited the practice: Sanchez-Albornoz in his
"Estampas de la Vida en Leon durante el Siglo X" quotes a Latin chronicle.
"Postquam illo rex Dominus Ranimirus (cui sit beata requies) divicit in
Simancas Abderracman (maledicat eum Deus) intravit in civitatem
Legionensem (quam Dominus salvet et diffendat)."

The Castillo Mofa at Medina del Campo

The tomb of Alfonso VIII of Castille

A siege engine

swoon", and ordinary decent folk in speaking of them habitually coupled them with sinners. There is a story of a good citizen who swallowed a reproof for supping with a civil servant, offering the somewhat lame excuse that he had reason to believe that the viands had been bought with honest money, earned outside his host's profession. As for ibn Abdun, who wrote a lively treatise on city government, he cannot find colours dark enough to paint them: malefactors, liars, black marketeers, the lees of society, shamelessly seeking to live on illicit profits and usury, amenable to bribes, unjust, perverse, without faith or religion. But ibn Abdun was a pessimist.

The exact make-up of the sovereign's cabinet—if one may so call it—is nowhere laid down except by one late author who gives a careful and inaccurate picture of the system obtaining in the good old days two centuries earlier. There were at an early date two secretaries—the word is *katib*—one of whom dealt with all correspondence, the other with finance; the latter's title is literally "master of the cash-book". Abd al-Rahman III reorganized the secretariat, dividing it into four departments: the heads of the first two dealt with letters from governors of provinces, one handling the frontier and seaboard, the other the interior. The third saw to the execution of decrees, the last looked after claims and petitions. All four had the title of *wazir*, which in most Muslim countries means "minister", but in Cordoba seems to have been a grade held by many officials who did not preside over a department of state. Its importance lay in the circumstance that it carried a certain rate of pay; and the impressive title of *dhu wizaratain*—master of two ministries—meant simply that the Caliph had been pleased to double the holder's emoluments.

The central administration was housed in the Alcazar at the Bab al-Sudda, the gate that opened on the river and the *rasif*, a paved gradient leading to the great bridge. This, the principal gate of the palace, was distinguished by a balcony, "without its like in the world", on which the sovereign loved to lean; sometimes it served as a penitential residence for an irresponsible prince of the blood. The entrance to the palace was by great folding doors, armoured with iron plates, on one of which was the famous knocker, a brass ring of exquisite workmanship representing a man's head with open mouth, which Hisham had brought back in 793 with the rest of the enormous spoils of Narbonne. Here the secretaries had their offices, which must have been very much like those in Constantinople a thousand years later, long rooms whitewashed and sparsely furnished

E

with a few divans and cushions, with piles of papers climbing up the walls, and a few officials squatting here and there on rugs, busily writing on sheets of paper held between the thumb and finger of the left hand.   These scribes were incredibly dexterous, writing from right to left with a reed pen, occasionally moistening a finger to rub out a word that might be improved on, and taking great care that the ends of the lines should climb towards the left hand corner, in accordance with the best models.

This was the hub of official Cordoba, its Whitehall and also its Tyburn; for it was also the traditional place of execution, and the gibbets that lined it were rarely untenanted.   Trophies from victorious campaigns were exhibited here for the public satisfaction: what sight more pleasant than a mound of Christian heads or the carcass of a pertinacious enemy?   The disinterred body of Umar ibn Hafsun hung there for years beside his son; and after the revolt of the *Arrabal*, which had come so near success, thirty-six of the leaders were crucified head downwards as a special mark of disfavour, besides a couple of hundred lesser traitors disposed in three neat files.

The extreme limit of ignominy was crucifixion between a pig and a dog.

Communication between the Sultan and his secretaries was through one of their number who had the entrée by day or night; he was known as the *hajib* or door-keeper, a title perhaps deliberately preferred to "*wazir*" to mark the break with the practice of the detested Abbasids.   In any case the word had lost its domestic significance (like "chamberlain") and now designated the highest minister of state.   He came immediately after the sovereign and was responsible for the entire administration, civil and military, though it was unusual for him to command in the field.   It was a post of enormous power, limited only by the ultimate sanction of dismissal and summary execution.   The Tarpeian rock was very near the Capitol.

Hakam I and Abd al-Rahman II both had the same *hajib*, Abd al-Karim ibn Mughaith, who had been the general of Hisham and so served in three reigns; while Hashim, the *hajib* and favourite of Muhammad, fell foul of his successor, Mundhir, who executed him and inflicted a prodigious fine on his sons.   Not all the Umayyads felt the need of a *hajib*: the greatest, Abd al-Rahman al-Nasir, had none during the second half of his reign: his son, Hakam II, revived the office, and by so doing prepared the end of the dynasty; for after his death it

was the *hajib* who ruled, first in the name of the shadowy
Caliph Hisham II and finally in his own.

The secretaries were recruited from the four leading Arab
families, but never from the royal house, which from motives
of prudence was excluded from any part in the conduct of
affairs. Only one commoner breaks into the aristocratic
preserve—one Badr ibn Ahmad, who had been freed by
Abdallah and filled many important posts with distinction. He
was the right-hand man of al-Nasir till 921. The Caliph was
also careful to counterbalance the influence of the Arab
notables by giving key posts in the administration to Slav
freedmen, of whose personal devotion he was surer.

The high-born Arabs were naturally jealous of their privilege,
and although they knew better than to argue with al-Nasir, they
had no scruple about crossing a lesser man. When Muhammad came to the throne in 852, he confirmed his father's
officers in their charges, but a year or so later his private
secretary fell ill and was temporarily replaced by a Christian,
Gomez ibn Antonian. On the death of the titular holder,
Muhammad, finding Gomez satisfactory, decided to give him
substantive rank, but being rather more of a bigot than most
of the Umayyads made the appointment conditional on his
changing his religion. Gomez made no bones about a public
profession of Islam, but the leading families took umbrage
and sent the Amir an indignant letter, containing a short list of
well-born Muslims who could as fitly have served him as
secretary. Muhammad picked one of them, a certain Hamid,
appointing him after a singularly casual test of his qualifica-
tions. He ordered him to draft a letter to the Warden of the
Marches instructing him to keep an eye on the great and enterprising clan of the Banu Qasi. On the advice of Hashim, who
was in the secret, Hamid galloped to his house, called his
friends together and set them to composing draft despatches,
finally copying out the best and presenting it to Muhammad in
the morning. Its exquisite phrasing won the Amir's approval,
and Hamid was assigned an official carpet in the palace:
whether he replaced Gomez or was supernumerary is not
recorded.

The senior posts offered unrivalled opportunities of corruption and were eagerly sought by those whose birth and con-
nexions were thought to qualify them for office. They set
about ingratiating themselves with the monarch, and it was
common practice for an ambitious magnate to make suitable
gifts to that end. In the Eastern Caliphate a case is chronicled

in which two rival candidates tendered for the post of *wazir*.   It
was at the end of the 10th century; the prince had to appoint a
successor to the *wazir* he had inherited from his father.   A high
official, having convinced him of his capacities by a well timed
gift of six million *dirhems*, was duly appointed, whereupon a
rival put forward the even more convincing argument of eight
million.   The prince, confronted with a problem where interest clashed with equity, arrived at an elegant solution not
unworthy of Sulayman ibn Da'ud: he cut both offers by two
million *dirhems*, pocketed ten million and appointed both.

Al-Nasir himself seems to have seen no harm in the custom,
probably esteeming it a sort of premium that candidates paid
to insure against a too unsympathetic scrutiny of their accounts.
The great Caliph was pleased to accept an offering from one
Ahmad ibn Shuhayd, a member of one of the Big Four clans,
and in due course was delighted to honour him with the rank
and emoluments of *dhu wizaratain*.   The gift is recorded in
detail by three chroniclers: the earliest computes it at five
hundred thousand *mithqals* of coined gold: four hundred pounds
of gold brick: two hundred sacks containing forty-five thousand *dinars* of silver: quantities of perfumes, musk and camphor: thirty bolts of gold brocade: five heavy tunics of luxuri-
ous materials: ten furs, including seven white foxes from
Khurasan: six silk garments from Iraq: forty-eight day and a
hundred night robes: a hundred sables: six tents for receptions:
forty-eight sets of harness of silk and gold: four thousand
pounds of silk yarn and one thousand pounds of raw silk: thirty
woollen carpets and a hundred prayer rugs: fifteen rugs of silk:
a hundred sets of ceremonial armour: a thousand shields,
one hundred thousand arrows, a hundred horses including
fifteen Arabs, five with brocade saddles, and five mules: forty
male and twenty female slaves: and finally a quantity of
flagstones and building materials.

At a later date ibn Khaldun, who claimed to have the list
before him, gives fuller particulars of the perfumes included in
this stupendous *douceur*: "four hundred pounds of aloes wood,
of which one piece weighing one hundred and eighty pounds:
two hundred and twelve ounces of pure musk: one hundred
ounces of pale amber, one lump weighing forty ounces: three
hundred ounces of refined camphor", used surprisingly as a
flavouring for stews.   Most of the other items are agreed with
slight embellishments, but the building material becomes a
villa for which the stone had cost eighty thousand *dinars*, with
twenty thousand straight saplings worth fifty thousand *dinars*

more. Ibn Khaldun also throws in "a very lovely Christian boy and a most beautiful maiden", besides half a ton of lump sugar.

A princely gift; Ahmad's servants must have been kept hard at it to recover the outlay from the tax-payer. However he had presumably gone carefully over the ground before investing his capital, and did not lack for relatives to consult. There was undoubtedly money to be made: another Shuhayd, Abd al-Malik, after nine years as Governor of Murcia had amassed half a million *dinars* in gold and jewels, besides landed estates. So much at any rate he offered Mansur in a desperate and unsuccessful attempt to escape retribution. Mansur was a great general and administrator and had a short way with transgressors in either field, perhaps because his own past was not blameless: and it may be surmised that he derived an additional satisfaction from the chastisement of Abd al-Malik, for although Mansur was of good birth he was a *novus homo* and not a member of the top-drawer families that had so long enjoyed a monopoly of the key posts.

The finances were administered by a number of treasurers, which varied with the royal pleasure. On one occasion al-Nasir dismissed the entire board of five and substituted four others, always members of the leading families: this was a revolutionary procedure and must have been occasioned by some exceptional mismanagement or transgression. The treasurers commonly gave proof of a sense of their obligations to the community and were quite capable of standing up to the sovereign. There was a famous conflict with Abd al-Rahman al-Wasit,[1] a patron of arts and sciences, when he gave the singer Ziryab a draft on the treasury for thirty thousand *dinars*, and sent a messenger with him to collect it. The senior treasurer, after first making sure that the others were in agreement, sent a firm refusal to the Amir. "Although we are called the treasurers of the Amir, (whom God preserve!), we are treasurers of the Muslims and collect the tributes not, by God, to waste them but to spend them on useful things. For this reason none of us desires on the Day of Judgment to see in his account that he took thirty thousand *dinars* from the Muslims and bestowed them on a singer for a couplet. The Amir must pay this from his private purse." Ziryab, whose artistic temperament did not preclude a lively sense of the value of his

---

[1] The three Abd al-Rahmans were distinguished by Arab historians as al-Dakhil—the Immigrant, al-Wasit—the Middle One, and al-Nasir—the Conqueror.

talents, said at once, "By God, but this is sedition," but the Amir "rightly esteemed their probity and gave them advancement".

It was easy for the sovereign to confuse the public and private purses, although the actual treasures were kept in different places—the Sultan's private fortune in his palace and the public monies in the *bait al-mal* in the mosque.   The basic public revenue was composed of the *sadakat* or alms, a contribution of one tenth of their movable property made by all Muslims: this was a religious obligation laid down by the Prophet and originally payable in kind.   This tax on true believers was balanced by the *jizya*, a poll-tax imposed on infidels, subjects by conquest, and the *kharaj*, a tax paid by owners of land in the conquered territories, when the terms of capitulation allowed them to keep it.   Other taxes were imposed from time to time, until under the Taifas the aggregate attained proportions which roused ibn Hazm to fury.

Miguel Asin Palacio translated his list: first the poll-tax, now extorted from good Muslims as well: secondly taxes on goods, cattle, pack animals, even bees: finally excise dues (roughly equivalent to the modern purchase tax) on everything sold in the market; even on wine, the sale of which is contrary to the law.   He calls the last an infamous scandal and a grave heresy; "by God", he exclaims, "if the tyrants thought they could attain ease by the worship of the cross, they would hasten to become Christians."

A further source of revenue was the land in conquered territory not protected by capitulation and so forfeit to the Muslim community, a large proportion passing to the sovereign. According to ibn Bashkuwal, al-Nasir drew an annual income of seven hundred and fifty thousand *dinars* from crown properties, which were mostly farmed on the share-cropping system: the farmers were called "halvers" but usually got much less than half.

There are several estimates of the total revenue of al-Andalus. Al-Bakri assesses it at six hundred thousand *dinars* under Hakam I (796–821), and five million four hundred and eighty thousand *dinars* under Abd al-Rahman III and his successors Hakam II and Mansur.   Ibn Haukal calculates that the state coffers contained twenty million *dinars* at the end of al-Nasir's reign, and twice as much in his son Hakam's time.   It is always a delicate business to assign a modern value to an ancient currency, since the variations in purchasing power are so great and so erratic as to play the devil with the most conscientious calculations: for although the *dinar* seems to have contained little more than half the weight of gold in the English sovereign, it was at that time possible for an average family at Mosul to live modestly for a year on twenty *dinars*.

However large the revenue, it is certain that the amount that reached Cordoba was only a fraction of that collected. In the first place, some taxes were farmed out to capitalists, and it was also the custom for provincial officers themselves to meet local expenses before remitting the balance to the capital. In spite of the opportunities for extortion afforded by these two circumstances, the pious historian would have us believe that the Umayyad rulers were extremely scrupulous in collecting taxes, and would not allow a single *dinar* to enter their treasury until ten of the most honourable residents had sworn that there had been no injustice or oppression in the collection.

If the *hajib* and secretaries were the most resplendent officers of state, the qadi of Cordoba was the most respected, and perhaps the only one to enjoy any measure of independence. In respect of the judicature, as in all other respects, the ruler was the absolute master, the fount of justice and the dispenser of authority: but in this one field he took careful account of public opinion, both in his choice of deputy and his behaviour towards him when chosen, treating him with real deference and never dismissing him unless exceptional circumstances forced his hand.

There is an extensive contemporary literature about the judges of Cordoba, their functions and their personalities. The historical method of the Arabs always inclined to anecdote, and the abiding interest of the people in these men, who constituted their last line of defence, found expression in numerous collections of the lives of the leading qadis [1] which afford an intimate picture of social conditions under the Caliphate.

The judge's title changed twice: the first was *qadi al-jund*—judge of the brigade, the *junds* being contingents from districts in the East, thus the Damascus *jund*, the Palestine *jund* and so on. A century later when a qadi was appointed who belonged to a family of local and eventually Christian extraction, which had embraced Islam but could not claim descent from any of the Syrian contingents, the title was changed to *qadi al-jama'a*—judge of the (Muslim) congregation. This appointment gave

1 The best source is al-Khushani's "Book of the Qadis of Cordoba", edited and translated by Julian Ribera and published by the Centro de Estudios Históricos, Madrid.

rise to dissatisfaction among the Arab clans, because the qadi's functions included leading the Friday prayers in the mosque in the absence of the monarch: this duty was therefore assigned to a *sahib al-salat*—prayer-master—of unquestioned Muslim ancestry.

Later still the eastern title of *qadi al-qudat*—judge of judges— came into use, on the eve of the collapse of the Caliphate, when the different services sought to mask a real decline in authority behind increasingly grandiloquent styles, such as wazir of wazirs, emblem of religion, trustee of the empire, and the like.

.   .   .   .   .

The qadi of Cordoba was neither a Minister of Justice nor a Judge of Appeal: he did not appoint or instruct other judges and rarely quashed a decision in another court. Ibn Abdun makes him the superior officer of the *zalmedina* and the police, but this was perhaps rather a pious aspiration than a statement of fact. He was however the guardian of the accumulated treasures of the *waqfs* or pious foundations, from which he could make grants to the Amir for purposes of public utility, to build a bridge or defray the expense of a campaign against the Christians. His high station was the reflection of his personal integrity, the universal conviction that he could be relied on, in the words of the modern formula, to do right without fear or favour, without affection or ill-will. He was as it were the incarnation of the sovereign's conscience, a limit that he deliberately set to his absolute powers; and there are not wanting examples of a qadi standing his ground in face of a sovereign's wish or express command.

One of the most striking, on account of the strong characters engaged, is the story of al-Nasir at the height of his power build-ing at his palace of al-Zahra a pavilion roofed with tiles that were plated with silver and gold. The courtiers invited to see this delicate fancy had exhausted the vocabulary of admiration: the qadi—the famous Mundhir ibn Sa'id—remained glumly silent. The Caliph asked him directly for his opinion, and he answered, "Never should I have thought that Shaytan had such mastery over thee, as to bring thee to the level of the infidels"—a dangerous reprimand to administer to a despot, even when backed by an apt quotation from the Quran prohibiting any such ostentation. But after a moment's acute tension, al-Nasir gave orders to strip the offending tiles and replace them with earthenware.

The law that the qadi administered was the *shari'a*, the Muslim canon law built on judgments delivered by the Prophet and commands embodied in the Quran. These were supplemented by "reliable"—*sahih*—traditions derived from the personal recollections of the Companions. When the code that had sufficed for the government of a small urban trading community was faced with the complex problems of a more advanced society, certain adjustments were admitted on grounds of equity—*istislah*—or argument from analogy—*qiyas*—or even on the basis of precedents, as in English case law; but the degree of elasticity varied widely in the four schools of canon law. In Cordoba it was the strict and conservative Maliki school that prevailed; its rigidity was tempered from time to time by the humanity of the qadi, which in turn reflected the independence of the Amir with regard to the *faqihs*, for they were never human and lost no chance of exacting the utmost rigour of the law, whenever they found the sovereign amenable, from either religious conviction or expediency.

Not all suits and disputes came before the *qadi al-jama'a*; he was relieved of most of the criminal and police work by various magistrates and commissioners of police, while Christians, Jews and other cattle were left to the devices of their own bishops and rabbis, with that sublime arrogance of Islam, which granted the capitulations to foreigners in the Ottoman Dominions, so assuring far-reaching privileges to the infidel states, simply because Muslims could not soil their fingers by dealing with such scurvy breeds.

The judicial *décor* was of the simplest: no *Palais de Justice*, no scarlet robes or wigs: the qadi sat in some convenient corner of the mosque precincts. One early qadi held his court in a passage on the upper floor of the mosque at the end of his street: others sat in their own houses, when they were big enough. He sat or squatted on a bench: his secretary and assessors sat or squatted near him.[1] Wherever he had chosen to set up his simple establishment, the hungry generation of lawyers hastened to rent chambers, to be within easy reach if the case called for a notary or sworn witness. The qadi carried under his arm a portfolio containing his scanty archives; and an usher or so completed the unpretentious apparatus of one of the most indispensable officers of state.

For the importance of the *qadi al-jama'a* was never in question:

[1] The Qadi had at his disposals expert advisers—*faqih mushawar*—whom he might consult on knotty points of law.

he ranked as one of the three pillars of the realm, with the all-but-autonomous Warden of the Marches, who held the northern frontier against the Christian kings, and the Admiral of the Fleet, who protected the seaboard from the enterprises of the Fatimid pirates from North Africa. His sentences were to all intents and purposes without appeal, for although in theory the Amir had to confirm sentences involving death or mutilation, and might upset a judgment or send it back for rehearing, in practice he was very chary of doing so, as the sequel might be a heavier sentence coupled with a request from the qadi to be relieved of his unwelcome duties. The qadi was in a strong position: many of those whose biographies enliven the pages of the "Book of the Judges of Cordoba" so far from seeking the post had done their best to refuse it. They were men of deep religious convictions: in hearing a case and pronouncing sentence they could not escape the apprehension that they were usurping the divine function; the responsibility of their position weighed heavy on them, and more than one longed for the time when he might mount his mule and go to the serenity of his home. One saintly man whom the first Abd al-Rahman wished to appoint refused and maintained his refusal in the face of urgent pressure from that redoubtable prince: another, whom the Amir Muhammad desired to make qadi for no better reason than a dream, in which he had seen the Prophet and the first three Caliphs gather round the man's sick-bed, declined point-blank and threatened to leave Cordoba if the monarch insisted. A third, learning that Hisham had in mind to offer him the post, at once shut his house and fled from the capital.

Muhammad ibn Bashir, when he had been superseded by the Amir, swore that sooner than again take office he would divorce his wife and set his slaves free: sure enough, when the Amir saw his mistake, he only succeeded in persuading Muhammad to resume his charge by compensating him fully for the domestic sacrifices entailed by his oath.

This qadi showed his indifference to public comment by his eccentric dress: he wore a saffron scarf and squeaky shoes (apparently a practice of dashing young men about town) and parted his hair in the middle like a musician—a degraded trade in Cordoba—so that litigants to whom he was pointed out as the judge thought their legs were being pulled. In spite of his sartorial misdemeanours, he was a man of the strictest principles and an unswerving minister of justice. Before he became qadi, he was gravely perturbed one morning, when the

Amir sent a crier round the market summoning all men holding goods of a certain Count Rabi to deliver them up within three days on pain of confiscation and death. As he held a pledge from the man, he went and took counsel with the famous *faqih* Yahya ibn Yahya, who answered by quoting the tradition, "A pledge must be restored not only to the just and honourable but also to the wicked and perverse." The Amir sending one of his servants to collect the Christian's property, ibn Bashir returned an uncompromising refusal, taking his stand on the *hadith* and adding that the injunction was particularly compelling in that case, for assuredly no-one was more perverse than Rabi. The incident is said to have led the Amir to appoint him when the place fell vacant.

He was a man with a proper respect for the soundness of his own judgments. On the death of one of the richest merchants of Cordoba, his slave came to the qadi and swore that before his death his master had freed him and told him to marry his daughter. The story being confirmed on oath by two Muslims on whose good faith ibn Bashir was accustomed to rely, he gave judgment accordingly. Not long after, one of the witnesses sent an urgent summons to the qadi; he was accompanying a funeral when he received it but went on from the cemetery. He found the man near death and in great pain, who dragged himself to the qadi's feet and said, "Unless you save me, I am going straight to Hell." "Not so," replied the judge, "trust in Allah and he will save you from the fires of Hell. What weighs on you?" "You recall that I bore witness in the case of So-and-so? What I said was lies: for the love of God reverse your decision." The qadi reflected in silence for a while; then putting his hand on his knees he rose and said, "You must go to Hell: my judgment stands."

Procedure was simple and summary. The respect paid by all to the judge was sufficient to keep order, but if there was any contempt of court, it was checked expeditiously by application of the whip. The parties stated their case or had it stated by advocates; supporting evidence followed, oral or written; the advisers were at hand, if the judge thought fit to consult them, in which case their opinion was put into writing and went into the archives. Judgment was then delivered, taken down and signed by the witnesses, and executed on the spot.

The Book of the Judges of Cordoba is full of instances of their impartiality and incorruptibility, their disregard of the powerful—ministers or even caliphs—in defence of the rights of the people, their personal austerity. They accepted no pay, and many lived in poverty: one returning home after leading the prayers in the mosque surprises a friend by fetching his bread from the baker: another is discovered kneading his own dough.   When Yahya ibn Masmar is dismissed, a friend sends a string of mules to carry his furniture, but Yahya, after distributing among his neighbours his prayer mat, his quilt, a water jar, a flour crock and a platter, which constitute his entire household goods, sends the mules back with his thanks and strikes out on foot for Seville.

There were judges who did not reach this high level: one was universally detested.   This was Yuhamir ibn Uthman al-Shamani, whose arrogance and discourtesy had left him without a friend.   One day when he was sitting, an enemy named ibn Shammar slipped among the names of the witnesses to be called a paper with the names of Jonas son of Matthew and Masih ibn Maryam (i.e. the Messiah son of Mary) and in due course the usher called them and continued to call them ever louder, until ibn Shammar intervened to inquire whether by any chance the Day of Judgment had dawned.   The same ibn Shammar wrote a lampoon on the judge's stupidity, which ends:

> The nape of your neck is shaven, but your face is veiled in darkness;
> Your brains are not worth a pennyworth of figs;
> May you live hated and languishing,
> And at your death may none grieve, and may you die an infidel.

Strong language, but by all accounts richly earned: so many complaints were received that the Caliph Hakam II held an inquiry into Yuhamir's fitness for the post.   Among those who gave evidence was one Giner or Janair, an old man of untarnished repute, who only spoke the Romance vernacular, although respected by all as a good Muslim.   He deposed that he did not know the judge himself, but heard the common people call him a so-and-so, employing an Arabic diminutive of such transcendent savour that Hakam said, "So saintly a man would not have used that expression had he not been constrained by his sincerity," and dismissed the qadi.

The Book of the Judges of Cordoba leaves an abiding impression of the fatherly lovingkindness of so many of them towards those who came before them.   So often they turn a blind eye to faults for which they deem the penalty excessive, drunkenness, for example, which was common in spite of the prescribed punishment of eighty lashes.   One judge engages in absorbing conversation until the tippler's weaving footsteps

have taken him round the corner. Another on his way home
in a narrow street and unable to avoid a delinquent approach-
ing with a tambourine in his hand and a suspicious sack on his
shoulders, (music is a serious offence), observes that he is a
judge and not a detective and walks on.

This compassionate temper is nowhere more apparent than
during the wave of religious exaltation that overtook the
Cordoba *mozarabes* in the middle of the 9th century, when many
of them courted martyrdom by publicly insulting the Prophet.
Instead of the summary execution which the law ordains, the
judges sent them to prison to give them time to reflect, or tried
to argue them out of their unwisdom, and only sentenced them
at last with reluctance. When the candidates for martyrdom
increased in numbers, the Amir called a synod of the Bishops, at
which he was represented by his secretary Gomez, "a man
indifferent in religion", to quote Gonzalez Palencia, "concerned only that the fanatics should not be confused with
Christians not so fanatical". In spite of the opposition of the
Bishop of Cordoba, the synod declared against the martyrs, but
the addiction could not be checked for seven or eight years,
until Eulogio himself, the principal advocate, himself achieved
a martyr's crown in 859.[1]

The labours of the qadi, then, were confined to civil matters:
crime and offences against public order were the business of
lesser magistrates. The organization of these services was so far
in advance of contemporary standards that the Christian
kingdoms that replaced the Caliphate retained it unchanged,
the Arabic titles passing into the Spanish vocabulary.

The principal officer in the city, corresponding roughly to the
French prefect, was called *sahib al-madina*—master of the city—
a title that was current for centuries after the fall of Cordoba

[1] The sentiment that kept the movement alive was less religious than
nationalistic, but the vogue of martyrdom was greatly encouraged by an
event of which the background was hidden from the martyrs. A priest
named Perfecto, who might have lived but for the treachery of the eunuch
Nasar, declared on the scaffold that Nasar would follow him within the
year. Nasar meanwhile had dipped into high politics: one of the Amir's
wives, Tarub, was so anxious that her son should succeed that she bribed
Nasar to give the Amir a poisoned draught, prepared by Harrani, the court
physician. Unable to deny the powerful favourite, Harrani pocketed the
thousand *dinars* bribe and made up the potion, but told a rival wife, who
lost no time in warning the Amir. He obliged Nasar to drink it himself as
a guarantee of good faith, and when the eunuch hurried to the physician for
an antidote, he was told there was none. The fulfilment of Perfecto's
prophecy may have inspired half a hundred martyrs.

in the form of *zalmedina*: he was assisted by the master of the market—*sahib la-suq*, in Spanish *zabazoque*—with specific commercial jurisdiction, and the chief of police, *sahib al-shurta*.

At one time or another the *shurta* was divided into great and little, "the high and the low justice"; there was even a middle *shurta* for a time. The distinction had nothing to do with the nature of the offence, but exclusively with the quality of the man in the dock: the little *shurta* looked after the '*amma*—ordinary folk—and the great *shurta* the *khassa* or aristocracy. And there was no egalitarian nonsense about the 10th century police in Cordoba: the treatment meted out to offenders was exactly equated to their social standing.[1] Ibn Abdun recommends that persons of social eminence should be treated leniently: is there not a *hadith* that says "Pardon those of high condition because to them a reproof is more painful than the whip"? Moreover their physical powers of resistance are slighter than those of the lower classes. But if they relapse the full penalty must be exacted.

Although the *zabazoque*'s province was the market, for the repression of fraud and counterfeit and the punishment of offences against hygiene, he was sometimes given far more extensive jurisdiction, and a grim little story in the Book of the Judges of Cordoba tells how at least one was invested with powers of life and death and instructed to use them without scruple. In the reign of Muhammad (an Amir whom the historians praise very faintly indeed) a terrible famine gave rise to a wave of serious crime, for which the punishment might be death or the amputation of a hand; such sentences required the confirmation of the Amir. Muhammad found this duty repugnant and authorized the *zabazoque*, one Ibrahim ibn Husayn ibn Asim, to impose and carry out the death penalty without reference to the Amir and without too nice consideration of the matter. Accordingly, whenever a prisoner was brought before him on a capital charge, Ibrahim would order him to dictate his will to certain ancients whom he kept handy to act as executors, and then had him executed without more ado. It happened then that some people brought in a young man who had been making a nuisance of himself, with the object of giving him a lesson, counting on the *zabazoque* to give him a good fright and at most a short spell of prison. Ibrahim asked the oldest and most respectable of the party what punishment he thought the culprit deserved, and the old man

[1] Under an edict of Caracalla, a similar distinction was made between the "honestiores" and the "humiliores".

answered "with exaggeration and extravagance and speaking metaphorically", 'he deserves that you should hand him over to these,' pointing to the platoon of executioners which Ibrahim had behind him. "Then Ibrahim ibn Husayn said to the old man, 'Go ye', and they went away. Then turning to the lad he said, 'Dictate thy will'. 'Oh! for the love of God', cried the boy, 'do not do this; my fault does not merit death and crucifixion'. 'The witnesses have affirmed to the contrary,' rejoined the *zabazoque*, and had him killed and crucified. When the party heard what had happened, they came to the *zabazoque* and protested that no evidence had been given in court of a crime deserving death; to which he replied, 'Did not he that spoke for you declare that he ought to be handed over to the executioners?' 'Nay, sir,' they answered, 'he said it by way of similitude.' 'Then the crime,' said the *zabazoque*, 'is on your heads, for not saying what you meant.' "

At the other extreme from this rough-and-ready conception of law, we find the advanced institution of the *sahib al-mazalim*, the Master of Oppressions literally, whose function it was to correct abuses of power by those in authority. When a complaint was brought against a noble or a high dignitary and the qadi doubted his own ability to enforce judgment or even compel the attendance of the delinquent—a situation that does not seem to have arisen very often—the sovereign could make a special delegation of his own supreme authority to the *sahib al-mazalim*, before whom the proudest had to bow their heads. Our own Court of Star Chamber was very similar in function, before it became the instrument of Stuart tyranny.

CHAPTER FIVE

FOREIGN RELATIONS

A THOUSAND YEARS ago, foreign relations were a personal matter between sovereigns, and the functions of diplomats were limited to conveying messages between royal cousins, although some latitude was usually left for a private haggle on terms. Ambassadors were *ad hoc* in the strictest sense of those overworked words: some centuries had still to run before Venice thought of establishing permanent missions abroad: if the Emperor of Rum had a proposal to make to the Amir of Cordoba, he chose the most adroit bargainer in his *entourage*, and posted him off with an impressive retinue and resplendent gifts, and left him to do his best. From the time the envoy set out, he stood on his own feet: no scrambled telephone lines inflicted the monarch's second thoughts on his representative. When he reached his destination, he had to be prepared to parry every manœuvre on the part of the other high contracting party, not excluding intimidation. Not seldom he faced a spell in prison, if his master's policy was more than usually obnoxious to the court to which he was accredited, though this was less of a hazard in 10th century Cordoba than later at Constantinople, where the Grand Seignior habitually confined ambassadors in a special prison suite at Yedi Kule.

At least once in Andalus diplomatic immunity was not respected. It happened at the very beginning, before the foundation of the Amirate. After his hairbreadth escape from the massacre of his family by the Abbasids, Abd al-Rahman made his way from the Euphrates through hostile Syria and Egypt to the Maghrib and crossed to Spain, taking up his quarters in Torrox with his Umayyad supporters, in the home of abu Uthman. The governor of Andalus, Yusuf al-Fikri, was inclined to come to terms and allow him to settle in the country; this plan, which might have changed the course of history, miscarried owing to the conceit of a member of Yusuf's embassy. There were three in the mission: Ubayd ibn Ali, his secretary Khalid ibn Zaid, and Isa ibn Abd al-Rahman, of the Umayyad clan. They brought with them a robe of honour, two horses, two mules, two slaves and a thousand *dinars*, together with a tactful letter, in which Yusuf recalled the benefactions his grandfather had received from the Umayyads, and offered Abd al-Rahman a lavish allowance and his daughter in marriage. When they were nearing Torrox, Isa, who seems to have been an unworthy clansman, persuaded the others to leave him in charge of the gifts, and not to hand them over before receiving Abd al-Rahman's formal acceptance of the offer; so Ubayd and Khalid went on alone to abu Uthman's house, where Abd al-Rahman was waiting with a group of his partisans. After Ubayd and Khalid had each delivered an oration, pressing Abd al-Rahman to accept Yusuf's offer of friendship, Khalid handed him the letter. Abd al-Rahman passed it to abu Uthman, saying "Read and answer according to my wish, which is known to you." They had in fact already made up their minds to accept similar terms, but Khalid, who had drafted the letter, "a very erudite and culti-vated man", according to the Akhbar Majmu'a, "but full of conceit and moved by vanity, which from old time has brought many to perdition in this world and the next", could not refrain from saying to abu Uthman, an old chieftain more used to the sword than the pen, "You will have to sweat, abu Uth-man, before you make your answer as elegant as the letter." "And abu Uthman rose and threw the letter in his face, and said, 'I will not sweat, you dog, much or little, nor will I answer it: seize him.'" So they fettered him, and when Ubayd protested told him that he himself was the ambassador, but "this is a ruffian who has come with insults and provoca-tions, the son of a whore and a renegade". Khalid remained in bonds during the ensuing hostilities, a prey to conflicting disquiet, for Abd al-Rahman put him in the charge of two wounded clansmen, with orders to make an end of him if the battle was lost; and Khalid did not know what to pray for, for victory was death and defeat was ruin.

Khalid's self-satisfaction was largely professional pride; the ability to turn an elegant despatch was one of the first quali-fications for a diplomatist: more than once the *hajib* issued orders to pay the closest attention to style, and prescribed penalties for such crimes as slipshod expression or writing on inferior parchment. It was a point of honour with the great to correspond in the most refined manner, employing rhymed prose and mazy metaphor and archaic turns of phrase. Kings were not above enticing one another's secretaries away by offers of rich reward: Mu'tamid so tempted a *wazir* of the King of Almeria, who came on a mission to Seville: and when Yusuf al-Tashufin sent Mu'tamid to captivity in Agmat, he hastened to take over Mu'tamid's private secretary.

F

It was expected of Caliphal ambassadors that besides a perfect command of Arabic, which involved first of all an intimate
knowledge of the poets, they should be proficient in Spanish
and Hebrew, and versed in the contemporary sciences, in
particular logic and dialectic, for they might well be called on
to maintain their sovereign's dignity in one of those full-dress
disputations so dear to the mediaeval mind: equally indispensable were a ready wit and an unruffled temper.   Much less
emphasis was laid at that time on the representational gifts—
birth, wealth, good looks—by which the Renaissance set so
much store, though they are mentioned with approval when an
envoy happens to possess them: nor was it expected that the
envoy should be able to drink the court under the table, as was
later essential in certain Scandinavian countries:[1] what was
sought was an acute and trained intelligence, not easy to find
among a feudal aristocracy whose time was fully occupied with
temporal pursuits; only churchmen and Jews had the leisure
for organized studies, and consequently ambassadors were commonly recruited from those two classes.   Oddly enough they
were not so mutually exclusive as might appear, for there were
Jews that were converted to Christianity and rose high in the
Christian hierarchy.   Burgos had two bishops who began as
Jews, of whom one had been Chief Rabbi in Burgos itself
before his conversion.   This was however some centuries after
the Caliphate collapsed: meanwhile the greatest of the
Muslims, Abd al-Rahman III, made no bones about employing
a Jew who was no Muslim.   This was Hasday ibn Shaprut, the
Caliph's physician, whom he sent on a mission to King Ordoño
IV of Leon, and in the twofold capacity of physician and envoy
to old Queen Tota of Navarre; he also leant heavily on his
talents when receiving embassies from Constantine of Byzantium and Otto the Great of Germany.

This insistence on elegant and fastidious style in diplomatic
exchanges did not preclude an occasional excursion into more
vigorous idiom.   Two notes which have been preserved from
the early days of Islam show that plain speaking also had its
advocates.   The first is from the Caliph Umar to Heraclius,
and asks for the release of a prisoner.   "In the name of God,
the Clement, the Merciful.   Praise to God, Master of the Worlds.
The blessing of God on his Prophet.   The servant of God,
Umar, to Heraclius, Emperor of the Greeks.   As soon as this
letter comes to thee, fail not to send me the Muslim prisoner

[1] Sir Percy Loraine once reported with some complacency an all-night
sitting with Mustafa Kemal.

who is with thee, Abdullah ibn Hudafa. If so thou dost, I trust that God will lead thee by the good road; but if thou dost not, I will send thee those that will not be turned aside from the road of God by traffic or bargaining. Salvation and felicity attend him who follows the straight road."

The letter reached Heraclius at a moment when, worn out by his victorious campaign against the Persians and already suffering from the dropsy that killed him, he was in no condition to take up the gauntlet; the prisoner was released.

At a later stage in the intermittent warfare between Byzantium and Islam, the first Nicephoros, having seized the throne from Irene, thought himself strong enough to refuse the tribute which she had been paying to Harun al-Rashid, and told him so in an insolent letter. Harun's reply is a model of compact vigour. "In the name of God, Clement and Merciful. Harun al-Rashid, Commander of the Faithful, to Nicephoros, Roman dog. I have read thy letter, son of an infidel: my answer thou shalt not hear but see." It was not long before the smoke of burning towns and dreary trains of fugitives made his meaning clear.

.   .   .   .   .

The first recorded exchange of embassies has come down as an entertaining if slightly fanciful account of the envoy's journey to the country of the Fire-Worshippers—*Majus*—by which name Arab historians refer to the Norsemen. Lévi-Provençal, in the course of his tireless study of the manuscripts in the great Mosque of the Qarawiyin at Fez, established that the exchange was in fact with Byzantium and took place in 839–840. The Byzantine Emperor Theophilos sent one Qartiyus, a name which may conceal the title of an official (cartularius?), to negotiate a treaty of friendship with Abd al-Rahman II. Theophilos at the time was hard pressed by the Abbasids on his eastern and southern frontiers, while his dominions in Italy were threatened by the Aghlabids in Sicily; and he had to put up with the depredations of a pirate dynasty in Crete, founded by the rebels who had been expelled from Cordoba after the revolt of the Arrabal. He sought to arouse Abd al-Rahman's sympathy by recalling how the Abbasids had massacred his ancestors, and to ingratiate himself by referring to the Caliphs in Bagdad not as Ma'mun and Mu'tasim, the official titles they chose at their accession, but as ibn Marajil and ibn Marida, sons of slave mothers. This highlighting of the servile origin of the Abbasid caliphs probably missed fire, for Abd al-Rahman's own forbears had had no prejudice against union with slaves: his response in any case was courteous and friendly but quite non-committal. It was entrusted to the distinguished poet Yahya ibn al-Hakam al-Bakri, who was so lithe and handsome that they gave him the *lakab* or nickname of al-Gazal—the Gazelle; and withal "endowed with a subtle and prompt understanding, and surpassing courage and spirit, and one who knew how to come in and go out by all doors".

The account of his journey does not tally with Constantinople any more than with Normandy: al-Gazal set out from Silves in the Algarve in a ship furnished with all requisites and suitable presents: Qartiyus took another, and after weathering a great tempest off Cape St. Vincent (where they were seriously off course), they proceeded to one of the fire-worshippers' islands to repair the damage, and then set sail for the King's residence "in a large island in the Ocean, three days' sail from the continent. There were multitudes of Magians, and many islands great and small, all inhabited by Magians: they had been pagans but were now become Christians." They were shown royal hospitality, but the Emperor was set on making al-Gazal bow to him, in spite of the understanding that nothing of the sort would be expected. To this end the Emperor had had a special low doorway cut into the throne room, which would oblige him to stoop, but al-Gazal "sat him down on the floor, and supported on his hinder parts and helping himself with his feet, he so passed the threshold and rose when he came into the royal apartment".[1]

The Emperor had assembled a great show of arms and treasure to impress the ambassador, but he refused to be impressed and embarked at once on his oration, and presented his master's letter and the coffers containing the gifts of brocades and costly vases, which gave great satisfaction to the King, and earned for the Spanish mission the most devoted service in their lodging. He specially made friends with the natives, "confounding their wise men in disputations and distributing heavy blows among their best warriors". His prowess came to the ears of the Queen, who sent for him. "When he came

[1] It is related, but I cannot vouch for the truth of it, that in the eighteen-thirties the Sultan of Turkey set a similar ambush when our envoy, Lord Ponsonby, presented his credentials. Lord Ponsonby rose (or rather stooped) to the occasion by bending over at the waist and entering backwards, presenting to the assembled dignitaries an immaculate expanse of white kerseymere.

to the presence, he bowed to her, then gazed at her for a space like one overcome by amazement". She asked through the interpreter whether it was because he found her lovely, "or perchance for the contrary reason!" He had his answer all ready. "I have seen our King surrounded by women chosen from the fairest of all the nations: yet none of them approached thy beauty". The conversation developed round this gratifying theme, and at length the Queen consented at al-Gazal's request to assemble the most lovely women of her country for his inspection. When the time came, "after studying them attentively from head to foot", he delivered judgment. "Verily they are beautiful, yet not to be compared with the Queen, for her beauty and other graces cannot be rightly esteemed except by the poets", backing his verdict with an offer to compose a poem on the subject, which would be recited in all Andalus. The Queen jumped for joy and offered him a present, but he refused, explaining that though it was magnificent, and any gift from the Queen would be a signal honour, yet she had already bestowed the most excellent gift in her power in allowing him to look on her, and if she wished to show him more favour, then let her receive him again. The Queen asked no better, and sent for him every day, "inquiring about countries and customs and histories", and when he left sent him gifts of woven fabrics and perfumes.

Lévi-Provençal's manuscript bears out much of this somewhat idealized account of al-Gazal's mission, and in particular his *succès fou* with the Empress Theodora (whose name the chroniclers turned into Nud): it seems he even broke through the enveloping protocol of Byzantium to get her and Prince Michael to visit him in the Marble Academy, where he was lodged.

It is a little saddening to record that when his friend Tammam ibn Alqama asked him whether the Empress was really so lovely, he replied, "Surely she was not ill-favoured, but truth to tell I needed her advocacy". But he did enshrine the story in a fourteen-line poem (which I have not had the opportunity of reading) so it is still possible that the wound in his heart was deeper than strict diplomacy required.

.   .   .   .   .

The next seventy years in Andalus were disturbed by internal troubles; the three successors of Abd al-Rahman II were hardly able to hold their own against the many rebels who established independent rule in outlying parts of their dominions: there is no record of embassies despatched or received. But when the third Abd al-Rahman had schooled his undisciplined subjects and turned his attention to the Christian kings on his northern marches, the Caliphate entered on the most splendid century of its history and came to be acknowledged as at once the most powerful and the most enlightened state in Europe, and a country to be courted by near neighbours or distant sovereigns. The Umayyads had never dropped their claim to the Eastern Caliphate, but it was not till Abd al-Rahman III the Conqueror had formally assumed the title of Caliph and Commander of the Faithful, that their name was mentioned in the Friday prayer and the *mihrab* in the great mosque of Cordoba was proclaimed the *qibla* to which all good Muslims should bow.

Ten years before this decisive step was taken, the Emperor of Rum had recognized a rising star and sent a friendly embassy. Nothing is known of it beyond a casual reference in a 14th century gazetteer of Andalus: in the description of the town of Lorca in the province of Murcia, of which a number of marvels are rehearsed, the following passage occurs. "And the oddest of odd things is the olive tree that grows in the neighbourhood of the castle of Sarnit, which is outside Lorca, and this is an olive tree in the Convent of the Mountain; and when it is the time of the afternoon prayer of the vigil of the first day of May the tree flowers, and night has not fallen before the fruit sets, and morning comes not but the fruit is black and ripe. And this is known to great and small, and they have watched it". Alas! the inevitable sceptic *did* watch it at a later date and reported that it did nothing more than reflect the colour of the morning, noon and night: but we know better, and so did the Emperor of Rum. For Ibrahim of Tortosa relates that in the year 917 the King of Rum told him that he purposed to send an embassy to the Lord of Andalus with gifts, and that among the chief of the favours he would ask was one relating to the convent where the olive tree grew and which held the bones of a martyr, who enjoyed the high esteem of Allah the Great and Powerful: "and I will ask him to make easy the manner of life of the people of that church and tenderly entreat them, so that they leave me the bones of this martyr, and if I succeed it will be the greatest boon on earth".

Lorca had other wonders; there was a gold locust that on some homoeopathic principle warded off locust invasions till someone stole it; besides a pair of stone bulls that wise men had buried in the old time, and when they were dug up, the cattle were smitten with murrain. It is now a quiet tidy little town that has been a garrison for generations and generations, and is full of the escutcheoned town houses built in the 17th and 18th centuries by the county families that farmed in the district; and the memory of its wonders has utterly perished.

There is no means of knowing whether the Emperor of Rum got his martyr, and it is hard to assess his chances without knowing what he offered in return. On more than one occasion the Umayyads drew on Byzantium for workers in mosaic and master masons, but in 917 Abd al-Rahman had not yet thought of the palace of al-Zahra, and the great mosque was not enlarged in his time. He would hardly have given them the martyr *pour leurs beaux yeux*. The Muslims never thought the Greeks worth cultivating: they accounted them lions within their castles, eagles on their horses but women in their ships; "if they have an opening, quick to take advantage: but if fortune is adverse, they are like goats in climbing their mountains, and they run so fast that they do not see the ground".[1]

Another mission from Byzantium came to Abd al-Rahman III between 944 and 949: it was minutely described by al-Maqqari, a North African scholar contemporary with Mary Tudor, who compiled a history of the Western Caliphate, to which he gave the captivating name of "a Whiff of Scent from Green Andalus". The embassy was sent by the joint emperors Constantine Porphyrogennetos and Romanus Lecapenus, and its object was probably nothing more than a general exchange of courtesies. Abd al-Rahman was evidently well disposed, for as soon as he heard of the envoys' arrival at Pechina, then the principal port but now a cornfield, he despatched senior officials to bid them welcome and see that they lacked for nothing on their way to the capital. As they came nearer, they were met first by large bodies of troops in battle array commanded by several generals, and later by two high-ranking eunuchs of the palace, who had instructions to show them the highest honour, and escort them to the palace of the heir presumptive, which had been assigned for their lodging. Here they were left for some days, every precaution being taken to see that no-one, gentle or commoner, should communicate with them. The Caliph came himself to Cordoba to supervise the arrangements for the ceremony, which he commanded to be held on a certain Saturday in the Vaulted Hall of the palace of al-Zahra. He sat on a golden throne studded with jewels, flanked by five of his sons on the right hand and three uncles on

---

[1] As I saw in the lunatic campaign in Izmir in 1921/2.

his left. After them came all the chief dignitaries, ministers and chamberlains in order, and the sons of the *wazirs* and the subordinate officers in their appointed places. The courtyard was spread with sumptuous carpets, and all the doors and arches were hung with marvellous brocades. The ambassadors were introduced, and after exhibiting becoming amazement at the evidence of the Caliph's might and magnificence, presented the letter from the Emperors, which had been the subject of no less careful preparation. It was written in Greek on pale blue paper in letters of silver, and contained the list and description of the gifts which the Lord of Constantinople sent to the Sultan. It bore a seal of gold weighing four *mithqals*: on one side was the image of the Messiah, on the other those of the Emperor and his son. It was in a wrapping of cloth of silver, enclosed in a golden box adorned with a portrait of Constantine painted on rock crystal: and all this was locked up in a coffer covered with a tissue of gold and silver. The preamble read: "Constantine and Romanus, followers of the Messiah and Kings of the Greeks, to the excellent and puissant and noble and meritorious Caliph Abd al-Rahman, who rules the Arabs of Andalusia, may God prolong his Life".

To enhance the solemnity of the occasion Abd al-Rahman had commanded all his court poets and orators to attend, in order to celebrate in fitting terms the eminence of Islam and the glory and splendour of the Caliph's Empire, and to return thanks for the mercies of God displayed in the manifestation of the Faith and the humiliation of his enemies. To this end he had instructed his son Hakam to select a spellbinder capable of doing justice to the theme. Hakam chose an eminent *faqih*, one Saki Abd al-Barr, "a man of immense knowledge of rhetoric and deeply versed in the Arabic tongue", but he had scarcely spoken a dozen words when the "sight of the imposing assembly, the utter silence of all present and the splendour and magnificence of those about the Sultan's throne" struck him with spectacular stage-fright. His tongue clove to his palate, and he fell senseless to the ground. A *savant* from Bagdad, the guest of the Caliph and himself the author of several admired works, and universally regarded as "a prince of science and an ocean of language", was hurriedly called on, but after making the correct invocation to Allah was equally at a loss for words. The situation was saved by Mundhir ibn Sa'id, who jumped uninvited into the breach and made a speech "composed in prose and verse and considered till this day an unparalleled literary achievement", thereby earning the gratitude of the

Caliph and eventual elevation to the supreme dignity of Qadi of Cordoba.

On this occasion the psychological weapons employed by Abd al-Rahman to infuse alarm and despondency in his rivals recoiled on his own officers; but more often, if we may trust the records, they produced the desired effect. Their use was universal, each potentate employing what he considered the most efficacious methods. Abd al-Rahman had an unusual device in his palace. He received foreign missions in the great Hall of the Caliphate, with ceiling and walls sheathed with gold and eight doors of ebony and gold hung from pillars of marble and crystal; when the sun struck into the hall, the reflections from the walls were blinding. Somewhere in the ceiling was the unique pearl which the Emperor Leon had presented to the Caliph, while in the middle of the floor was a great laver of mercury, no doubt brought from the mines of al-Madan. When al-Nasir wished to startle one of his courtiers, he signed to a slave to stir the mercury, "and at once the whole room was shot with rays of light, which reduced those present to terror, as the whole hall seemed to be floating away, so long as the mercury went on quivering. The room seemed to revolve round an axis, as if it followed the movement of the sun". An optical illusion that seems improbable to one who has not been subjected to it. Al-Nasir, however, according to al-Maqqari, was so captivated by his pond of mercury, that he would not let anyone look after it but his son, Hakam.

The Tulunids had a similar pool of mercury in their palace at Cairo: it was fifty cubits square and had solid silver pillars at the corners: there was a bed of skins floated on it, anchored to the pillars by silver cords.

In the beginning of the 10th century the Caliph of Bagdad is said by Abulfeda to have undermined the confidence of ambassadors from the Emperor of Rum by a stupendous tree with eighteen gold and silver branches, with trembling leaves of divers colours. It stood in a pool of crystal water, and had silver birds in the branches. "The tree", says Abulfeda, "swayed like those in our forests and then was heard the song of all those birds." The Caliph had also a hundred lions, each with his keeper.

The Emperor of Rum for his part owned a prodigious throne that by means of a concealed mechanism could be raised to the ceiling. It was guarded at the four cardinal points by gilded lions that roared intermittently during audiences, opening their jaws and lashing their tails on the floor.

All of which seem less effective than the device of an eccentric old gentleman whom I knew in my childhood: he had an enormous drumhead hidden behind a curtain by his armchair, which he could strike by a potent drumstick set in motion by his foot. This he would set off without warning in the course of conversation with an unsuspecting guest.

Abd al-Rahman also exchanged embassies with Otto the Great, whose long reign so nearly coincided with his own, and who in bringing his factious German vassals to heel met and surmounted the same problems as beset Abd al-Rahman in Andalus. For once, Abd al-Rahman made the first approach, sending the famous Recemundo to Otto's court. The chroniclers record nothing more than the bare fact of the exchange: the only interesting feature is the personality of the ambassador and the enlightened tolerance of the Umayyads. Recemundo was the baptismal name of a highly cultivated Christian of Cordoba, equally proficient in Latin and Arabic, who was better known as Rabi' ibn Zaid: his diplomatic services were rewarded by the bishopric of Elvira; if the see was not technically in the Caliph's gift, he applied the system of a congé d'élire, which came to the same thing. Recemundo later carried out a number of missions in the Levant to procure precious objets d'art for Abd al-Rahman's palace, including a portentous sculptured fountain which he commissioned in Byzantium. It is doubtful whether he ever exercised any episcopal functions beyond drawing the emoluments: he must have been fully occupied with his diplomatic and artistic missions, under both Abd al-Rahman and Hakam. It is more than likely that he fetched the Byzantine mosaic workers who built the lovely mihrab of the Great Mosque.

At the end of his long reign, when Abd al-Rahman was universally acknowledged the most powerful monarch of his time, the Kings of France and Italy sought his friendship, and he was the arbiter of the destinies of the wrangling Christian dynasties of Northern Spain. As one embassy followed another along the road to Cordoba, the protocol of reception became increasingly elaborate. One that came from Catalonia a year or two before his death is described in detail by ibn Arabi, the famous mystic of the 13th century.

Impressive preparations had been made: the three-mile road from Cordoba to al-Zahra was spread with mats, and lined with soldiers whose scimitars formed an arch over the envoys' heads. At the palace gate they were met by dignitaries dressed in silks and brocades, whom they saluted respectfully, thinking the Caliph was among them, but were waved on. From the gate to the court appointed for their audience their path was covered with brocades, and at various points richly attired officers were posted. Every time the envoys saw one of them, they prostrated themselves, imagining it was the Caliph, "but they said 'Get up; this is only a slave among his slaves' ". At last they found him in the middle of a sanded courtyard, dressed in simple clothing befitting his ascetic mode of life: "in short and cheap clothes", says Ibn Arabi, "all that he wore was worth four *dirhems*. He was seated on the ground with bowed head: before him a Quran, a sabre, and a brazier. 'There is the King,' they told the ambassadors, and they prostrated themselves before him. He raised his head towards them, and before they had time to speak, he said, 'Allah has commanded us to bid you to conform to this' (pointing to the Quran); 'if you will not, we will constrain you by this,' (the sabre), 'and if we kill you this is the fire that awaits you'. He then dismissed them and they signed peace, accepting all his conditions."

This embassy was treated with exceptional severity and confined to its lodgings: Otto's envoys had been allowed to attend the church of St. Martin on feast days.

Another of al-Nasir's ambassadors, who also served Hakam, was the Jew Hasday ibn Shaprut, who combined skill in diplomacy with medical science. At one stage in the perpetual fratricidal wars in the north, King Sancho of Leon had been ousted by a group of feudatories, who claimed that his extreme fatness made him unfit to reign, and put Ordoño the Bad on the throne. Sancho took refuge with his mother, the spirited old Queen Tota of Navarre, and sent a plaintive appeal to al-Nasir; who, seeing the profit to be drawn from civil war in Leon, sent Hasday to Navarre. He prescribed a treatment that reduced Sancho to decent royal proportions, and brought the entire family back to Cordoba, where the Caliph extorted ten castles from the unlucky Sancho as the price of his support. This however he gave without stint, so that before he died he saw Ordoño a fugitive, and Sancho master of Leon and Castille and his vassal.

Seven years later Ordoño came in his turn to beg for Hakam's assistance. Al-Maqqari tells the story of the interview: it seems that Ordoño was so desperate that he came unannounced: "seeing that all his devices had miscarried, the accursed infidel bethought him to repair to al-Hakam without asking leave or making any stipulation". In spite of this lapse, a guard of

honour was provided; and when he came near to the Bab
al-Sudda, he asked in his desire to please where was the tomb
of al-Nasir, dismounted, removed his cap and prayed fervently
on his knees. Two days passed before he was accorded a
reception with full protocol, troops in battle dress, Slavonian
guard in full regimentals, the doctors and *faqihs* and poets in
attendance, *wazirs* and chamberlains in their proper places,
and Hakam on the throne in the eastern hall that opened on the
terrace, with his brothers and nephews around him, and the
Qadi of Cordoba, that Mundhir ibn Sa'id al-Balluti, who had
saved the day on the occasion of Constantine's embassy to
Abd al-Rahman III.

Ordoño was introduced, wearing a tunic of white brocade of
Christian manufacture and a jewelled cap; his party were so
dazzled and bewildered by the troops lining the approach that
they crossed themselves in amazement. At the outer gate
Ordoño's suite dismounted; Ordoño himself rode on as far as
the Bab al-Sudda, the gate that opens on the river opposite the
bridge, a favourite place for gibbets and executions. Here he
was seated on a raised platform with cloth of silver, until Hakam
sent for him, when he walked to the Eastern Hall. The
splendour of the assembly was such that he halted and took off
his cap and cloak, believing the Sultan to be among them, but
he was beckoned on to the throne, which he approached with
the utmost humility, kneeling, rising and advancing a few paces
before kneeling again, until he reached Hakam, who raised him
by the hand and set him on a seat draped with cloth of gold.
One has little sympathy for Ordoño: a man who in those times
earned the *sobriquet* of *el Malo* would hardly have expected any.

However his ostentatious subservience paid dividends.
Hakam agreed to help him, and gave him a robe of honour, a
tunic and gown of cloth of gold with a belt of pure gold set with
pearls and rubies, his retinue also receiving gifts according to
their rank. Hakam's policy of supporting both sides in an
infidel quarrel also paid dividends: it was not long before
Sancho saw the storm-clouds gathering, and sent an embassy to
reaffirm his acceptance of Hakam as overlord and promising
to carry out his undertakings to Abd al-Rahman III, which
success had driven from his memory. When he handed over
certain castles on the frontier, Ordoño was put off, and dis-
appears from history.

The lesson was not lost on the other Christian kings; Catalonia and Navarre hastened to make submission: the great
Fernan Gonzales, Count of Castille, sued for peace; from as

far away as Galicia Count Rodrigo Velazquez sent his mother as ambassador, whom Hakam received courteously and sent back loaded with gifts. During the rest of his reign Hakam was at peace, and able to give his time to the more congenial pursuit of science and literature and the formation of his noble library.

.   .   .   .   .

Behind such diplomatic courtesies stood always the ultimate sanction of war, and it was never long out of the thoughts of the rulers of Cordoba. The northern frontier, if not in a state of permanent war, was at any rate fully mobilized. It was divided into two Marches, Upper and Lower, the former having its headquarters at Zaragoza, the latter at first at Toledo, and later, when the Caliphate expanded, in a more forward position at Medinaceli. At Zaragoza the *muwallad* family of the Banu Qasi or Banu Lupe had established themselves as hereditary Wardens of the Marches, and often under a weak ruler at Cordoba called themselves the third kings of Spain. They had a system of defence in depth, with castles as strong points, and carried on with the Christian princes on the other side of the frontier the same endless raids and forays that for centuries enlivened our own Scottish border. The Marches served as bases for the more serious campaigns; these were usually mounted during the summer in the earlier days of the Amirate, and depended on the state of the harvest, for the troops had to live on the country. Mansur laid down stores of corn and other supplies in good years, and so was rarely forced to forgo a campaign on account of a bad harvest.

The armies were at first recruited on something like the feudal system, based on the *junds*, the tribal chiefs being expected to bring their contingents to battle in return for their fiefs. The defects of this system were first of all the lack of discipline and the propensity of the levies to fade away in times of stress, and secondly the danger that the loyalty of the tribes to their chiefs might outweigh their loyalty to the monarch. From the beginning therefore the Amirs balanced this force with a private standing army of mercenaries, composed of Christian slaves or *mamluks* (a word meaning a slave with a white skin as opposed to an '*abd*, whose skin is black). These were the Mutes, who figure so often in the chronicles, so called not because their tongues had been torn out, as was sometimes held by the Romantics, but because knowing no Arabic they could not communicate with the people of Cordoba.

These were afterwards given their freedom and formed a separate caste, known as the Slavonians from the origin of the first of them, which kept itself very much aloof from the population: they were the personal bodyguard of the sovereign, were always kept under good discipline by their officers, and made an altogether more reliable force. Later sovereigns increased the army by importing Berber and Sudanese mercenaries, and at the end Mansur carried out a complete reorganization on a territorial basis, and finally broke down the old aristocratic structure of the Arab tribes, which had given so much trouble to his predecessors.

Mansur's army had better discipline than hitherto: his men were steady on parade, and even the horses refrained from neighing. Any offence met with condign punishment. Once a man bared his sabre, and the glint of the sun on it caught Mansur's eye; he excused himself by saying he had pointed it sheathed at a comrade and the blade had slipped out, but his head was taken off in the interests of good discipline.

Even that army had something less than perfect morale. One day Mansur, filled with pride when reviewing them before a battle, asked the general, ibn Mushafi, whether there were not a thousand good fighting men there: that hardbitten veteran doubted it, and continued to doubt when the dictator reduced his figure successively to five hundred, a hundred, fifty and at last ten. Meantime a Christian champion had ridden out and challenged all comers, and disposed of three Muslims who picked up the gauntlet. In default of further volunteers, ibn Mushafi sent for a man of the Upper Marches, who presented himself mounted on a skeleton of a horse and carrying a water-skin. Ibn Mushafi told him to bring the Christian's head, whereupon first depositing his water-skin in his tent, he rode out and duly reported with the trophy. There were clearly so few real fighters, that the army commander knew them all by name.

By modern standards the armies were tiny. The Palace Guard was never more than five thousand strong: which seems to have been about the recognized strength of an army. It was divided into five battalions of a thousand, composed of five companies of two hundred, further divided into five troops of forty: these finally into five parties of eight. Two thousand would be mounted. Before setting out on a campaign the King would hold a review, either pitching his tent (*suradik*) in the plain, or if there was room, in the courtyard of the Alcazar. The night before, there was a solemn ceremony in the mosque, when the standards were distributed. There is a spirited poem describing Mu'tamid's departure to the wars: the courtyard is filled with fluttering pennons, the Indian sabres flash, noble steeds with skins like satin stand in pairs, one for the master, the other for his squire. The drums beat, the signal is given, the troops move off, while the spectators weep tears of blood.

Strategy was simple: the army marched into the enemy's country, cutting down his crops and fruit-trees and driving off his cattle. In a full-dress war when armies met, it was customary to agree a day for a pitched battle, although it was anything but unusual for one side or the other to break the agreement and get their blow in first; it was such a *ruse de guerre* that gave Abd al-Rahman I his victory over Yusuf al-Fikri. In defeat the army melted away, and the retreating commander would find himself left with nothing more than a handful of cavalry round his diminished banner. The first reward of victory was the loot of the enemy's camp: one fifth went to the sovereign, while the remainder was apportioned *pro rata* among the rank and file. There was one class of soldiers whose only pay was this share of the spoils: these were the *mujahids* or *ahl al-ribat*, who were crusaders and volunteers in the holy war: the rest all drew pay and rations.

Siege operations were protracted, and commonly resolved themselves into a contest, which party could hold out longest against starvation. In the siege of a strong town, the sovereign might build a permanent town in the neighbourhood, from which to maintain the siege during the winter: this was the method of al-Nasir before Toledo and Fernando and Isabel before Granada: the latter's city of Santa Fé still bestrides and strangles the main road to Malaga. The defenders were reduced to great extremities, and would get rid of useless mouths by putting the aged and feeble out into the moat; they might be taken and sold as slaves, but as they would hardly fetch a *maravedi* in their emaciated condition, it was more usual to leave them to perish under the eyes of their townsfolk. When the starving garrison was near giving up, a parley was often held, and agreement made to surrender at a certain date if relief had not arrived in the meantime.

War was carried on in Spain with more regard for humanity than may appear. When prisoners were slaughtered, it was to point a particular moral, not as in France a matter of routine. During the great crusade that ended in the victory of Navas de Tolosa, Alfonso VIII outraged the large French contingent which had helped to capture Calatrava and wished to slit the

throats of all the captives. Alfonso, in accordance with the
local rules, refusing to allow any such thing, the French
marched back home; on the way they wished to relieve their
feelings by killing all the Jews in Toledo, but were again
thwarted by the townsfolk.

There was a certain etiquette between foes: it was a hard
school, but both Muslims and Christians had some respect for
the rules, in particular in the case of an enemy who had earned
the reputation of a good fighter. The Chronica Adefonso tells
the story of the end of Munio Alfonso, who at the beginning of
the 12th century was alcalde of Toledo, which Alfonso had
taken in 1085. He was a valiant fighter and had held the pass
against the Moors for many years. In 1133 the Lords of
Cordoba and Seville mounted a full-scale expedition against the
town, and led an immense host to the attack. Munio Alfonso
assembled his army at the Mata de Montiel, heard Mass and
made his prayers to our Saviour, the Blessed Virgin Mary and
Santiago of Spain, and awaited the onslaught. The victory
was his, the two kings were killed, and immense booty taken.
He had their heads chopped off and set on pikes; "then he
sent and had their bodies wrapped up in magnificent silken
cloths, and set in a meadow to be taken away in the care of
certain Saracen prisoners". He met his own fate eventually
in a battle where he was hopelessly outnumbered; as the result
was not in doubt, he ordered his stepson away, with the words,
"Take care of thy mother and our sons: I do not want us both
to die to-day", but he had to drive him off at the point of his
lance. Then he and his small party climbed to the top of the
Peña del Ciervo and fought to the last man. The Saracens
cut off his head, his right arm and his leg below the knee, wrapping what remained of the body in clean shrouds and handing
it over for burial. The arm and leg they hung on the highest
tower in Calatrava: the head they sent to the mothers of the
two kings, and at last to Yusuf al-Tashufin.

The Chronicle ascribes his defeat and death to his inconsider-
ate and sinful action in killing his daughter, "whom he had had
in legitimate wedlock", because "*jugaba con cierto joven*"—she
sported with a certain young man: instead of recalling to mind
the treatment his Master gave to the woman taken in adultery.

A century or so later even more distinguished courtesy was
shown to a bonny fighter by the Moors, who were in revolt
against Alfonso el Sabio. The Governor of Xerez, Garcia
Gomez Canillo, had been attacked unrelentingly by night and
day, until at last he and half a dozen squires, all that remained

A Muslim raid

Muslim war
standard

(*Above*) The Church of
Santo Cristo de la Luz
at Toledo

(*Left*) The Church of
Santo Cristo de la Luz
at Toledo, interior

on their feet, shut themselves up in the keep of the alcazar and fought till all were dead except the Governor, but he refused to surrender. The Moros had such great admiration for this doughty warrior that they would not kill him, but fetched ladders and hooks, and so caught him and dragged him out alive.

From such grim narratives it is a far cry to the second campaign of Enrique IV in 1457 against the Moors in Granada.[1] On arrival at Alcala la Real he dismissed his levies and marched towards Jaen. "Thence he commanded two thousand two hundred horse to march with him to Cambil, and took with them the Queen, who went on a palfrey well appointed, and with her ten damsels mounted in the same manner, of whom half wore Moorish tunics and the others brassards and very tall plumes, so that some belonged as it were to the men-at-arms and the others to the cavalry. And so with these people the King and Queen came so near to Cambil that they seemed disposed to assail the fortress, and when the Moors saw them approach they manned the ramparts; and the Queen called for a ballista, which the King gave her all armed, and with it she took a few shots into the Moors. And this game finished, the King returned to Jaen, where the knights who knew how to make war and were accustomed to it mocked and jested, saying, that that manner of war was rather against Christians than Muslims. Others said 'Without doubt, this is how the Cid made war in his time'. "

The sport of Kings, in Mr. Jorrocks' words. Here indeed was the image of war without its guilt, and even less than twenty-five per cent of its danger.

[1] Moshe Diego de Valera, "Memorial de Diversas Hazañas", quoted by Juan de Mata Carriazo in Andalus XIX 2.

G

CHAPTER SIX

POETRY

The Arabs have always had a sensitive ear for verse and music, and the simplest of them are at home with quarter-tones, and can catch a metrical pattern too subtle for any but the most exquisite western ear. Arabic is a rich and flexible language, and the Arabs counted it an indispensable part of a gentleman's equipment to possess an exact and extensive mastery of words. This way of thinking has had a corresponding influence on the fabric of the language, which has become an object of the most refined study: grammar, which in the West is rated a mean and pedestrian subject fit for elementary schools, has always been held in great esteem by the Arabs, a grammarian ranking as high as any other literary figure.

The grammarians start from the postulate that the language is perfect, even as the Quran is perfect and not susceptible of error, and that no part of it falls short of the standards laid down by divine inspiration. Whatever in other languages would be cheerfully labelled "irregular" they therefore cleanse from any such inadmissible taint by concocting a rule to fit it. The minutest attention has been lavished on structure and the interrelation of form and meaning: it is theoretically possible to take the three letters that form the root of most Arabic words and modify them in any of fourteen ways to express the finest shades of meaning. The vocabulary moreover is itself extremely rich; the curious have counted an infinity of words signifying "camel" or "lion"; though this is perhaps not quite so surprising as it may seem to a race not intimate with lions and camels; but after all the list of English words for "dog" may very likely be as long, if one includes all the breeds one meets at Cruft's and their show points. While any Englishman except a professional dog-fancier would be satisfied with those appropriate to his own dog, an Arab of average instruction would be mortified, if he failed to appreciate all the delicate distinctions affecting camels or lions that might get into a poem. Whether the less cultured among them do in fact take in such subtleties or whether they are just carried away by the musical rhythm of the verse, I have never been quite sure; but there can be no doubt about the emotional response.

Poetry then has always been the Arabs' hobby, and the poets

always enjoying the veneration of the multitude, their works have been preserved from the earliest days. There is a famous set of seven poems called the Mu'allaqat, which are regarded as the foundation of any anthology. The word means "hung up", and the explanation usually offered is that these seven poems were so perfect that they were written in gold on Coptic linen and hung up on—or even in—the Kaaba. Recent theories however discount the truth of this legend and assert that they were collected in the 8th century by a rhapsodist or reciter called Hammad, who bestowed the title of al-Mu'allaqat on the collection, an explanation that does not take us much farther.

The poems all date from the 6th or early 7th century: they are concerned with tribal rivalries—one poet boasts of the prowess of his own tribe; another spits defiance at a rival chieftain (whom he afterwards killed); the choice of subject is natural, almost compulsory; it is that of our own early ballads. There is however this difference, that while in our own later literature such a ballad would be a conscious—even self-conscious—imitation of an archaic *genre*, in Arabic literature for centuries after poets were required to conform to the earliest models, in both form and subject.

The classical *qasida* or elegy is a long poem that keeps the same rhyme throughout: lines, or at least couplets, must be complete in themselves; *enjambement* is not permitted; it is therefore not uncommon, as the poems were orally transmitted, for the order to be noticeably varied. It was even admitted that whole slices of earlier poems in the same metre might be incorporated. The framework of the *qasida* is equally stereotyped: the author riding through the desert with a friend (or more classically two friends) halts at an abandoned camp site and mourns the absence or death of those he has known. This allows him to expatiate on the charms of his beloved, and allied topics: one of the most usual is an exhausting journey he has made, which introduces the excellence of the horse or camel on which he made it, or even his car, nowadays. He finally passes to the real subject of his poem, which is the glorification of the patron who has commissioned it, or abuse of one of his enemies.

This restricted choice of theme and the rigid frame in which it is confined effectively fettered inspiration and drove the poet to conceits and artifices, comparisons and metaphors: Garcia Gomez has happily described the classical muse as less lyrical than algebraical.

The interminable harping on these desert topics had little

interest for the new class of city-dwellers, that came up as the Empire expanded. These men were no longer Bedaween, and the desert and dead camp-fires and fast camels and the lost beloved no longer set their pulses racing; and as poets derived their income from wealthy patrons, they were obliged to conform to the latter's tastes. In Spain, as soon as the Andalusian grew out of his first naïve respect for the cultured East, the poets chafed under the classical shackles and chose more homely subjects, and more congenial to the opulent townsmen. Palaces, gardens, orchards, *fêtes champêtres* and walks along rivers that wind through wooded valleys—these provided the new frame in which they presented their variations on the absorbing themes of love and wine; they also invented at a later date the charming genre of the *nawriyyat*, flower poems, that flourished at Mansur's court.

Such was the stock-in-trade of the bard of Andalus; but even so equipped his road was not without pitfalls. For one thing the Prophet had evinced a marked aversion from the poets' trade: he had had Umar kill a poetess named Asma, of the tribe of Aus, for writing lampoons after the battle of Badr; and when he occupied Mecca, one of the four persons excepted from the general amnesty was a singing-girl, whose performance had given currency to a similar satire. He had perpetuated his dislike of poets in a somewhat obscure passage in the Quran:[1] "Shall I tell you on whom the demons descend? They descend on all the guilty impostors and teach them what they have learned in the heavens. They give ear, but most of them are liars. They are the poets, who are followed by men led astray by their passions. Dost thou not see how they go wandering in the valleys and say otherwise than they do?" It is not known what poets he had in mind, but the majority of those that came after him certainly lived up to his charge of insincerity. A poet will sing a rhapsody on wine and drop into prose to affirm his lifelong devotion to water, or respond to an ardent epistle with an equally spirited declaration, which he will send by a slave instructed to inform the receiver that the convention obliged him to reply in this manner, but his real intention is precisely the contrary.

[1] Sura XXVI 221 ff. This long sura, entitled 'al-Shu'ara'—'the Poets', was designed to rebut the assertion of Muhammad's opponents that the Quran was just poetry, and to show that it was the work of a prophet. For this reason it recites the stories of Moses, Noah and other prophets, the only explicit reference to poets being the passage quoted, which comes at the very end.

If one may judge by the unbroken succession of poets and the limitless quantity of verse that they produced, the religious disfavour remained ineffective, except at the outset of the Almoravid and Almohad dynasties, before their primitive puritanism wore off. A story is told of Yusuf al-Tashufin, at a feast given by Mu'tamid, listening to a *qasida* in his honour and not understanding a word of it: another of Abd al-Mu'min fidgeting during the high-flown eulogies of a distinguished court poet, and at last cutting him short with a "Silence, poet, you bore me." Their indifference to verse was probably not all religious: they were Berbers and would lack any intimate knowledge of the literary language; there are no further instances of similar recalcitrance, even in the Berber *taifas*. In general the poet had a clear field; his talent might open a quick road to affluence and honours, though his early struggles might be painful.

Poets were indispensable in an age when the Press had not been invented, and statues and pictures were contrary to the Faith. There was no better medium than verse for propaganda and advertisement: an effective panegyric would be absorbed into the tenacious memories of all who were present at the feast when it was delivered; and they would relay it to gatherings of their friends, when they returned home. A pungent epigram on a rival would earn a rich reward: for there are few things more quotable and easier to remember. Only the author must beware of ever entering the sphere of influence of the subject of his satire: poets had lost their eyes for less. A story is told of abu 'l-Makhshi, a leading poet in the days of Abd al-Rahman I, who wrote some verses in praise of the Amir's son Sulayman; a fanatical adherent of Hisham, another son of Abd al-Rahman and rival of Sulayman, deeming that the verses contained a slight on his master, kidnapped the poet and removed his eyes. Abu 'l-Makhshi had no remedy but to compose some affecting verses on his blindness and recite them to the Amir: who after inquiring into the circumstances awarded him a thousand *dinars*, twice the *thar* or blood-money to which he was entitled.

The apprentice poet, like the apprentice craftsman in Europe at a later date, spent his *Wanderjahre* travelling from one court to another, earning a precarious living. He arranged his time-table so as to spend his night at the expense of a prospective patron; almost any township or village held some person of consequence who would pay for a *qasida*. The great nobles and kings even maintained a permanent lodging for itinerant bards, and a billeting-officer (*sahib al-inzal*) to attend to their needs. Some of the kings even had a special at home day for poets: it is recorded by Pérès that Mu'tadid of Seville assigned Monday for their recitations. They were treated with scant ceremony until they had made their mark, and given a poor place in the list of precedence, coming after chess players, head gardeners, vets, doctors and astrologers: they were at least provided with a stool during their performance, which in the highest circles was given in an ambience of red: red shoes, red hat, red baize mantle—even a heavily rouged face. Their reward might be anything or nothing. There is a well-known story of ibn Ammar, who in his later years was hailed as the singer of the age, but in his youth was hard put to it to make ends meet. As he travelled he excited hilarity with his poverty-stricken accoutrements, a cap too small, a fur cloak too large for him, his scanty household effects in a pair of saddle-bags strung across an emaciated mule; his best efforts were rewarded with a night's lodging and a contemptuous bounty. One night at Silves he gave of his best to a local magnate, who sent him off in the morning with a bag of barley more appropriate to his faithful companion than himself. Some years later, at the height of his glory, when King Mu'tamid gave him the choice of any office within his dominions, he chose to return to Silves as governor, and after taking possession of his post with magnificent ceremonial, sent for his early patron and returned his bag stuffed with silver, telling him that if he had filled it with corn instead of barley, he would have got it back full of gold.

It was not only in Andalus that kings kept their poets on short commons, like hungry falcons that had to stoop on locusts. In France long afterward, when Ronsard was very famous, we hear of him begging his publisher for some firewood to warm his hands; it can hardly have been in earnest, unless the publisher carried out conscientiously the policy of his royal patron, Charles IX—a mean man—who had laid it down that poets, like horses and hounds, worked best when they were hungry.

So much for the professionals, who made verses to fill their bellies; but any gentleman might find the accomplishment a valuable addition to his armoury. An apt couplet, or even half a line, might open the gate of advancement or parry the sword of destruction. Half a hundred stories bear witness to the extreme susceptibility of Arab magnates to a neat quip in one of the sixteen classical metres. There is a story of three young bloods at Granada who were surprised in the middle of

their revels by the grim *wazir* Samaja al-Sanhaji, who dis-
approved of wine and was accustomed to punish drunkenness
by decapitation.   One of the three, though well in his cups,
had enough wit left to improvise three verses that saved their
lives.   In the same way a youth, who on the strength of some
eminence in literary circles had been given an appointment by
Mansur and used it to embezzle three thousand *dinars*, was
shackled in preparation for a flogging, but by means of two
happy impromptus succeeded first in getting his shackles
removed and then in escaping scot-free.

It was this knack that made a queen of a slave-girl.
Mu'tamid was strolling in the Silver Meadow, a popular
promenade along the Guadalquivir, accompanied by ibn
Ammar, his minister and favourite.   They were playing their
game of capping verses: Mu'tamid propounded a line describing the effect of the cold wind on the river, which made it look
like a coat of mail; ibn Ammar was slow to respond, and a girl
who was washing her clothes intervened.   Her quickness and
her beauty so enchanted the monarch that he bought her and
married her, and indulged all her caprices in the spacious
manner of the Thousand and One Nights.[1]   One morning
looking out of the window of the palace, she saw snowflakes
falling—a rare event in Cordoba, which hardly knows winter—
and bursting into tears, called Mu'tamid a monster and tyrant
for not taking her to some country where she might see this
lovely thing every winter.   So he had all the hills planted with
almond trees, so that every winter their blossoms should be a
substitute for snow.

It is pleasant to record that the romance lasted a lifetime:
she bore him several sons, and when he was deposed by the
Almoravid conqueror, accompanied him into exile and is
buried by his side.

A successful poet must have an inexhaustible memory:
Pérès tells how the poet al-Abyad, despairing of solving a
knotty point of semantics, swore that like the great Farazdaq
before him he would rivet chains to his feet until he had got a
certain treatise by heart.   Hammad al-Rawi, the compiler of
the Mu'allaqat, had an equally retentive memory.   When
Walid, the Syrian Caliph, asked him why men called him the
Narrator, he replied simply, "I can relate all the works of all
the poets you know, and all those you have never heard of.
For every letter of the alphabet I know a hundred *qasidas*, and

[1] Her verse appears to have been the sensible suggestion that it would be
a finer coat of mail if it was solid.

all of them from the days before the Prophet." In spite of these staggering attainments, Hisham, the heir to the throne, took a dislike to him, and when he succeeded, Hammad went into hiding. After a year he thought it safe to reappear, and was at once summoned by the Governor, who had orders from Hisham to give him a racing camel to bring him to Damascus, with five hundred *dinars* journey money. When he arrived, he found Hisham in a large apartment floored with marble blocks, picked out in gold. He was seated on a red carpet, wearing a robe of red silk dripping with musk and ambergris, with two damsels wearing pearls of price in their ears. After inquiring after the poet's health, he said he had sent for him because a certain verse was running in his head, and he could not remember the author. Hammad at once identified it and recited the entire *qasida*. The Caliph was ready to jump for joy and told him to name his reward: the poet asked for one of the girls. "Both are thine", replied Hisham, "with all their jewels and apparel", and in addition ordered the treasurer to pay him a hundred thousand *dirhems*.

.   .   .   .   .

To the western mind a great deal of this verse is intolerable: so much is frankly admitted by the experts. No-one is better qualified to pass judgment on this subject than Garcia Gomez, who unites profound scholarship with a very delicate feeling for poetry; and in an essay on a late poet, ibn Quzman, he points out how in Arabic literature all the emphasis is on artifice: stiff rhymed prose, similes, metaphors, conceits, mannerisms. There is a lack of warmth and humanity: it is all a dreary masquerade, where smiles are pearls, eyes are violets, flowers are jewels, rivers are swords. Indeed as the student toils through the translations of Pérès or Schack,[1] he is crushed by the frightful uniformity of so much of it: the loved one's waist is eternally compared to a branch rising from a heap of sand: the poet is a bird whose plumage is so bedewed by the patron's generosity that he cannot fly away: the lightning in the rain is like the fire of the poet's love among his tears. More than half of it is *cliché*; the celebrated improvisers had only to dredge up tags from their retentive memories. Some weary student used the epithet "pickled": Garcia Gomez has a kindlier reference to "delicious literary arabesques and verbal Alhambras", thinking perhaps of the acres of stucco decoration where the same *motif* is repeated without respite.

[1] More exactly Valera's version of Schack.

Yet the Arab could be moved to ecstasy by the sheer music of the verse. In his "Poemas Arabigo-Andaluces" Garcia Gomez quotes the account of a certain Arqami calling on a singing-girl, a slave called Ajfa. He found her in a squalid lodging, the only furniture two broken stools and two divans with their stuffing protruding. The singer was wearing a Harat dress that had been yellow but had faded with frequent washing; her feet were crusted with dirt. But when she sang, the visitors fell off their divans with delight; Arqami threw off his tunic, seized a quilt and put it on his head, crying out like a Jew praying. His friend rose and took a basket full of bottles of olive oil, balanced it on his head and danced until the bottles fell in all directions, to the dismay of the owner. A fantastic scene, but there was every excuse: the slave's talent was so remarkable that Abd al-Rahman I afterwards paid a stiff price for her.

It is very difficult to arrive at a just estimate of so delicate a subject. After a longish course of study, it is tempting to agree with that Dutch candidate for honours at a German university in 1831, whose thesis was entitled "Qui vero poetas Arabum propter ipsorum prestantiam legat, si non sensu carere certe otio suo abuti videtur." "Anyone who reads Arab poets on account of their excellence, if he has not lost his senses is undoubtedly misusing his leisure." My own command of Arabic has never been sufficiently advanced to enable me to extract the sweetness from Arabic verse in the original. Inevitably I must miss much of the bouquet, though I sometimes suspect Garcia Gomez and Pérès of making up the deficiencies of the originals from private stores of lyrical inspiration. However, when one is struggling with an unfamiliar medium, and particularly when it is as abstruse and recondite as Arabic verse, it is easy to lose one's sense of measure and criticize the fashions of one age by the standards of another. The Elizabethan era, which we are accustomed to admire without reserve, had a great relish for the conceits which we find tedious in the Arabs: and to tell the truth, we find them tedious in the Elizabethans. Lyly's "Euphues" touched off a consuming passion for whimsies that lasted half a century, and there were few more hardened offenders than the Virgin Queen herself. On the whole, the Arab poets compare not unfavourably with those "English apes and very zanies" who, in Drayton's vigorous words,

imitating his ridiculous tricks,
So spoke and writ, all like mere lunatics.

Some of their conceits were pleasant enough.

" The roses are scattered in the river, the passing winds have spread them
   with a breath;
  As if the river was the corslet of a hero, wounded by a lance, with the blood
   flowing from the wound."

Or

" The river is like a papyrus on which the zephyr writes;
  When the lovely manuscript is spread, the branches bend down to read it."

Or

" Give me no other songs than the neighing of chargers: that is my music:
  Lay on the burning soil my saddle for my bed, the waving banner for my
   tent."

Or

" My heart is a stool at her feet."

It is all a question of degree.   Here is a poem on a quince by
al-Mushafi (10th century), which I have translated from Garcia
Gomez's rendering.

" When it stood in fragrance on the branch, and the leaves had woven for it
   mantles of brocade,
  I stretched out my hand gently to pluck it and place it like a censer in the
   middle of my room.
  It had a robe of ashen velvet that fluttered on its smooth golden body,
  And when it remained naked in my hand except for its narcissus-coloured
   shift,
  It brought to my mind One I cannot name, and the ardour of my yearning
   withered it between my fingers."

To ears accustomed to "preciosity" this would be an exquisite
poem: to those brought up half a century ago it is rather cloy-
ing: a "modern" would dismiss it with contumely.
Take again this sharply etched picture of a cock greeting the
sun:

" To proclaim the death of night the cock arose, decked with a poppy,
   rolling the sparks of his eyes;
  The Emperor of Persia must have given him his crown, and Mary the Copt
   her earrings."

That would still be admired, if Christopher Marlowe had set it
to rhyme: indeed a famous Spanish contemporary of his wrote
something very like it: the cock becomes a lascivious spouse,
"canorous cryer of the sun, bearded with coral, crowned with a
turban of purple, not of gold."

But it can be overdone:

"Torrents of aromatic oil have flooded the Valley of Stones: it is the news of his coming".

"The wing of darkness departs before the dawn; like a crow that takes wing uncovering white eggs".

"A negro swam in a pool, whose waters did not hide the stones beneath; The pool was a blue eye with a black pupil".

"The night is a sea, where the stars are the foam, The clouds the waves, the crescent moon a ship".

When such comparisons are the mode, poets have some excuse for pushing their technique to its utmost limit: even poets like ibn Hazm, who has moments of tenderness that would earn him a place in the Golden Treasury. Yet he opens a parenthesis in his Collar de la Paloma to boast that he has compressed into a single couplet similes of three, four and five sets of objects. Here he compares three sets:

"The dew, the cloud and the scented orchard Seemed our tears, our eyelids and her cheek."

His supreme effort on drinking wine in the dark with a girl covers five sets:

"I, she, the cup, the white wine and the darkness Were as earth, rain, pearl, gold and jet."

Even the forbidding subject of Grammar is pressed into service; ibn Hazm, describing someone's magnetic quality, writes

"My eyes cling to you wherever you go, as the adjective follows the noun."

Another poet produces a vivid picture of two lovers enlaced like the *Alif* and *Lam* of the definite article. These are two parallel vertical strokes, which are intertwined in the highly decorated Kufic inscriptions.

All very mannered, and a survival from the days when poetry was an aristocratic profession. In Muslim Spain, however, the tormented 11th century marked a great change; poetry blossomed on all sides, in the cottage no less than the palace: the Muse touched the lips of many who had never had leisure to attend lectures or commit to memory the repugnant mnemonics that were the nearest thing to a university education. The countryside teemed with natural poets, singing with unconscious art very much in the manner of the Lake Poets centuries later. Towns acquired a reputation for poetry, as others for pottery or embroideries. In the little city of Silves on the coast of the Algarve, young and old lisped in numbers: it was all Daphnis and Chloe over again.   The geographer Idrisi in the book he wrote for the Norman kings of Sicily, after commenting on the elegance of the buildings and the well stocked markets, remarks that the inhabitants excelled in eloquence and in quoting poetry, high and low being equally gifted.   Here Mu'tamid spent some of his early years and must have absorbed some of the spirit of the place.   But in the whole of Andalus the Muses were abroad.

.   .   .   .   .

"Emotion recollected in tranquillity": emotion was certainly not lacking in the 11th century; to begin with the *fitna*, "the troubles", when the Caliphate foundered in bloody riots, and the palaces were looted, so conclusively indeed that their sites were lost: when one ruler cut down another and was cut down in his turn; and yet, as in the early days of the French Revolution, sometimes the millenium seemed to have dawned. One Caliph surrounds himself with a galaxy of poets and philanthropists, who last but a few weeks before making way for a less idealistic *camarilla*: an elective republic is founded at Seville, from which an Empire is born, with Mu'tadid cast for the role of Napoleon.   Little kingdoms spring up on all sides, the *Reyes de Taifas* hold courts steeped in culture, in the intervals of fighting for existence against Cordoba and one another. There is enough emotion to inspire a dozen epics and untold *qasidas*.

Yet the subjects the poets choose are rustic and pastoral: their medium is pastel rather than oil: never the violent midday light of summer; their delight is spring or autumn, evening or sunrise, or the warm southern night with moon or stars peering confidentially through the trellises at the meetings of friends or lovers.   They drop easily into a gentle melancholy, a sort of twilight nostalgia: they are oppressed—and not unnaturally— by a sense of the passage of time, the futility of pleasure, the instability of fortune and the uncertainty of the hereafter.   So in the later years of Muslim Spain, much of the old trappings of insincerity and artifice drops from the poet's shoulders; his quest of silence and reflection is genuine; as he writes, so he lives, not only turning aside from gathering rosebuds but even discarding those once gathered: ibn Ammar for example methodically sets out to destroy his Juvenilia.   The approach of age leads many to abjure their youthful follies and take to a life of asceticism.

Pérès traces this attitude, which is neither Arab nor Muslim, to the Celt-Iberian blood which ran in their veins: if I had less respect for his massive scholarship, I would like to have put a little of it down to the Jew, who lives and moves in the future: who fixes his eye on the Promised Land, and however he lives in the present, never loses sight of what one day shall be.

The political intrigues and agitation of the 11th century throw the poets on their own resources: most friendship is feigning; man is more perilous company than a starving wolf: friends are cordial till you need help, and then doors are bolted. Therefore avoid the society of the great; better solitude, tempered by the company of books.

"The guests have departed," says the poet,

" Solitude is my friend, a book my companion,
  A companion who will not weary me nor betray my friendship nor wrong
      me."

How better spend one's old age than withdraw to quiet study and plain living, in endeavour to efface the record of past naughtiness? A favourite subject with the poets, though not all: one impenitent old gentleman thinks otherwise:

" I subdued my passions while young, but when Time whitened my hair,
  Oddly enough I gave them the rein. Would God had granted me to
      begin with old age and grow younger!"

With such rare exceptions they are very conscious of their precariousness of tenure, and seek safety in seclusion: listen to abu Ishaq of Granada: [1]

" They asked me; do you not want a fine mansion that would make others
      jealous?
  I answered: No. A cottage suffices a wretched mortal.
  Where it not for winter and the burning dog-days of summer, and the need
      to keep thieves from my bread,
  And women to defend, I would build a house no more enduring than the
      spider's."

Classical artifice is given up: poetry becomes human, and I suppose a little Victorian. The sight of ruined palaces brings a lump to the throat: the following, one of many lyrics on this subject, has the additional interest that it comes from the pen

[1] Pérès p. 459.

of Muhy id-Din ibn al-Arabi, a grave scholar and the greatest
mystic of his century.

> " On the edge of the terrace there are houses that glitter in the sun,
>   But have no inmates and are in ruins;
>   Little birds mourn in their rooms,
>   Sometimes silent and sometimes singing.
>   I spoke to a little bird who was chirping,
>   With sadness in his heart and disconsolate.
>   Why dost thou sob and lament? I said;
>   He answered, For a time that has gone never to return."

Love is treated with a new simplicity.   Ibn Hazm, who in
his catastrophic career had "tasted the most diverse pleasures
and undergone the most varied fortunes", wrote

> " They asked me my age, seeing white on my temples.
>   I said, After mature thought I account I have lived one moment.
>   To her who owns my heart I gave a kiss one day, by surprise;
>   However many years I may endure, I have only lived that moment."

"Jenny kissed me" six hundred years before Leigh Hunt.
And who that has once loved has not known the longing he
expresses in these lines?

> "I were content, could I but take a knife
>   And cleave my heart and set thee safe inside,
>   Locked in my breast as long as I should live;
>   And when Death took me, there shouldst thou still rest
>   Heart of my heart until the judgment day."

Here finally is a lament for Mu'tamid, by ibn al-Labbana,
who had enjoyed his bounty and did not turn his back on him
in his ruin:

> " I shall forget everything before that morning by the Guadalquivir, when
>   they were in the ships, like dead men in their graves;
> The people crowded on both banks, watching how those pearls floated on
>   the froth of the river.
> Veils fell, because maidens no longer cared to cover their faces, and faces
>   were torn, as mantles were in the old time;
> The moment came: what tumult of farewells! damsels and gallants vied
>   in lamentation:
> The ships went accompanied by sobs, as a lazy caravan which the
>   cameleer urges with his song.
> Ay! how many tears fell into the stream!   How many broken hearts those
>   galleys carried off, unfeeling! "

.   .   .   .   .

Side by side with this poetry, still classic and elegant in spite of its fresher outlook, there had meanwhile grown up a new measure, that some scholars assert modified the whole trend of European prosody. This was the verse form called technically *muwashshah* or double-rhymed, or more commonly *zajal*, which just means a low song. It is said to have been invented by a blind poet, Muqaddam of Cabra: more probably he took a popular form, already current, and gave it definition. In spite of its somewhat complex structure, it seems to have come as naturally to that generation as the Limerick to ours, though its rhyme systems are far more elaborate. It broke completely with the rules: the lines are half as long as the classical models; instead of one rhyme from start to finish, they follow a number of fixed patterns, and accent replaces quantity; the language is the vernacular, dropping case-endings and mingling Romance words with Arabic: and the whole group of stanzas that compose the poem is clinched at the end by a couplet, called the *kharja*, which must be in the vulgar tongue, either Spanish or Hebrew. It was written to be sung rather than recited, and as the singer designed to pass the hat round, the subjects chosen were light and cheerful like our own music-hall songs, but also frequently scrofulous, to cater for the debased taste of the street-corner audience.

Chance has preserved a song-book containing a hundred and fifty *zajals* by a poet called ibn Quzman, who lived in Cordoba at the end of the 12th century, when the little kings had faded out and the grim Almohads were ruling. We know a good deal of him from his works:[1] he came of a good family, had had a good education, was tall, fair and blue-eyed, had an unkind wife and was quite certainly a bad hat. He knows that his verse is fresh and gay. "*Me vino un zejel que parece miel*"—"I caught a song as sweet as honey": he has a short way with his inspiration: "*Ven, laud maldito, ayudame*"—"Come cursed lute and help me"; and celebrates instead of nectars and the like plain wine—*manzanilla* or *añejo*. His instructions for his burial are characteristic: "Let me sleep with the vine between my eyes; wrap me in its leaves for a shroud, and on my head a turban of the same."

Scholars who have compared the structure of these *zajals* with the metrical forms used by the early troubadours have allied to Ribera's theory that the origin of Provençal minstrelsy is to be sought in Spanish folk-songs, and more precisely in the *villancicos*, that were sung "in canon" by the farm hands. The

[1] See Garcia Gomez's masterly study in "Cinco Poetas Musulmanos."

objection that from Andalusia to Provence is a long journey for a verse-form to make, is not to my mind very formidable.   Contact between Spanish *jongleurs* and their Provençal *confrères* was frequent in those days and not too arduous: they all lived the same gipsy life, and every Andalusian *virtuoso* spoke both Arabic and Romance, and would have little difficulty in getting on terms with a member of his own craft.   I have seen mechanics who hardly knew a word of one another's language exchanging ideas with surprising facility: poets and musicians speaking allied dialects would have had no trouble at all.

Admittedly the contents of ibn Quzman's Cancionero are far less edifying than the early *villanelles*, but he flourished in a degenerate society, and there is reason to believe that much of the lost earlier *muwashshahas* were as full of idealism and *amour courtois* as the first Provençal lays.   After all, the conception of chaste love was a Muslim invention, and was well established in Spain by the 10th century.

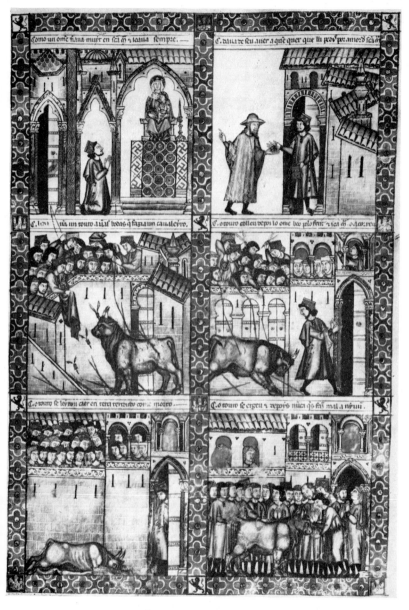

The Miracle of the Bull

The frontispiece of the Bible of Alba

CHAPTER SEVEN

SLAVERY

Like many, indeed most brilliant societies before and since, the Amirate of Cordoba stood on a foundation of slavery, which underlay every department of public and private activity. At the head of the state the Amir relied on an army composed of slaves to maintain the northern marches against the incursions of the Christian kings and to curb the factiousness of the Arab aristocracy at home: the wide estates, that were the principal source of his private treasure, were cultivated by slave labour, under the supervision of slave overseers: the officers who presided over the administration of his dominions were mainly recruited from slaves who had grown up in his palace. The domestic side of his life was organized by a literal army of slaves, so numerous that each sovereign that succeeded to the throne was obliged to abandon his predecessor's palace to his womenfolk, and build a new one for himself.

The Amir's manner of life was imitated by his subjects within the measure of their resources, and indeed is still in fashion in Andalusia, where a fairly rich man will employ a dozen or more servants under an *ama de casa*, and a small bourgeois as many maids as he can get at a hundred pesetas a month, bringing his daughters up to be charming but quite useless in a kitchen. To many people in England the hours of labour and the wages received would be accounted a survival of slavery, but such slaves as I know seem content with their lot and even attached to their oppressors. I fear this will not last much longer, as the prevailing tourist boom has brought too many misguided foreigners into the south of Spain, and the rank weed of "democracy" will soon have choked the natural comity of employer and employed.

The condition of a slave in al-Andalus was far removed from that of a slave in Rome. Severity and cruelty were by no means unknown: in a moment of exasperation, the poet-king Mu'tamid pitched a singing-girl into the river, where she drowned; but there is no record of an Arab patrician habitually throwing erring slaves to his lampreys. On the contrary, an intelligent slave might reasonably look forward to freedom, even if he refused to deny his faith, though it was far easier if he accepted Islam; the annals of the Caliphate are powdered with the names of eunuchs who rose to influential posts in the palace,

or commanded armies and fleets. Such success stories can be
found in Byzantium also, whence eunuchs were introduced into
Andalus, but the rigid structure of the Empire of Rum did not
afford the same *carrière ouverte aux talents*.

For a gifted female slave the road to power might be far
shorter. Competition however was stiff, and there was a very
large entry. The Patio de las Donzellas in the Alcazar at
Seville is said to derive its name from the annual function held
there, in which the Sovereign collected a tribute of one hundred
choice girls. No doubt similar ceremonies took place in other
centres, and there was a constant supply of slave-girls of such
outstanding quality that a dealer would offer each one
separately. A pretty face and figure, though indispensable,
were not in themselves enough: the girl had to present intellectual attractions as well. So far as concerns physical beauty,
the points of a slave were as exactly tabulated as those of a
horse or a pedigree dog to-day. There were official tables of
graces which enhanced, and blemishes which reduced, the value
of the merchandise: notaries worked with such formularies at
their elbows in drawing up the contract of sale, and several
have come down to us from markets in various cities, Toledo,
Cordoba, Algeciras. Inspectors were assigned to the slave
markets to arbitrate or adjudicate in cases of dispute, having
full regard to the purpose for which the slave was acquired.

Among male slaves, for example, Berbers were esteemed for
farm work, Catalans as craftsmen, Byzantines as mariners. On
the female side, white slaves were at a premium, though for
summer service Nubians were prized for their fresh skin, and
were relatively sterile in a colder climate than their own. The
colour bar played no significant role except when the purchaser
intended to breed from the slave: in such cases the pedigree of
both parents was called for, and after the contract was concluded, if it was established that one of the parents had black
blood, the deal was cancelled.

The ruling house had a liking for fair white women from the
North and in particular for those "platinum blondes" that not
so long ago were unkindly derided as tow-haired; Aurora the
Basque, famous in history and drama, was only one of a multitude whose hair had that ashen tint. In consequence of this
predilection, the royal house came to be mostly fair, with large
blue eyes. That their subjects shared their tastes is evident
from the formularies: in these, white slaves, (who commanded
the highest prices), are always described as Galician; that
little kingdom at the northwest corner of Spain, never con-

quered by the Muslims, was peopled with Celts, who grew up
in a climate in every way similar to that of Ireland and acquired
Irish good looks. If Galicians were prized for their com-
plexions, Catalans were thought more intelligent and accounted
better breeders, but all things considered, Galicians took pride
of place in the slave market, and had the additional bull point
of speaking a language already current in most homes.

The Umayyad Caliph Abd al-Malik ibn Marwan, who ruled
at Damascus in the 8th century and was not above inscribing
his name on his predecessors' works, laid down a broad rule for
the guidance of amateurs building up a harem: for temperament, take a Berber: for a fine and numerous progeny, a
Persian: for good housekeeping a Rumi. This may be compared with another more detailed specification left by a dealer,
who designed his model slave with much the same finicky precision as a cricket enthusiast to-day picking an ideal All England
side. This expert propounds a Berber girl, captured at the
age of nine, taught in Medina three years and three more in
Mecca, and at sixteen taken to Iraq for the ultimate polish.
For there was a steady demand for accomplished slaves, and
the *cognoscenti* paid extravagant prices for the best models. A
singing-girl once fetched thirteen thousand gold *dinars* [1] in Iraq,
where by general consent the most agreeable tone prevailed,
another Iraqi girl named Qamar—Moon—was bought at an
incredible figure by Ibrahim al-Hajjaj, an opulent grandee and
governor of Seville, and there introduced the refined Iraqi *ton*
and a becoming appreciation of the classical poets.

This was in the early days of the Amirate, when the Andalusians still regarded Iraq with the reverence due to the leading
school of manners, and singing-girls from that country exercised
in Cordoba an influence comparable with that of a film-star in
our own day. If exquisite manners were the stamp of Iraq,
Medina was the school of deportment and solid attainments:
moreover the Medina graduate was slim and graceful, quick-
witted, soft-voiced and *espiègle*. There were three of them,

---

[1] At or near that time a poor family could just make ends meet in Mosul
on twenty-five gold *dinars* per annum. Five thousand *dinars* was a respectable fortune: it is related of a certain prodigal that after running through
one fortune he inherited forty thousand *dinars*, and somewhat unexpectedly
reformed. He spent one thousand *dinars* on repairing his father's house,
which had fallen in, seven thousand on the purchase of furniture and three
slaves for the long-suffering parent, laid out two thousand in commercial
ventures, buried ten thousand for emergencies, and spent the remaining
twenty thousand on an estate, where he led a virtuous life.

named Fadl, 'Ilm and Qalam—Grace, Knowledge and the Pen—who between them for long held the unstable affections of the second Abd al-Rahman,[1] and each bore him a child. The third was a Christian from Navarre, who had been captured in her childhood and polished in Medina: she had the additional quality of a fair complexion, not to be acquired in the holy city.

By the 11th century Andalus had grown out of its early respect for the eastern tone, and anthologists were irreverently praising local poets and disparaging the classic masters. This new self-assurance was reflected in the training of singing-girls, who were now imported from Bagdad and Medina and given their final polish in Cordoba, where the best finishing schools were to be found. A prospectus has been preserved for us by ibn Bassam, issued by an Andalusian doctor of medicine named ibn Kinani, who conducted a successful school for singing-girls, taking advantage of his professional *entrée* to the best houses to push his superfine wares. He claimed that he could awaken intelligence in stones, let alone homespun peasant wenches. "Know that I now have in my house four Christian girls who yesterday were dolts, but to-day are instructed in Logic, Philosophy, Geography, Music, Astronomy, Astrology and the use of the Globes, in Grammar, Prosody, Literature and Calligraphy." This claim, he asserted, was substantiated by learned essays they had published, interpreting obscure passages in the Quran and also such abstruse matters as the Bedouin practice of meteorology. His young ladies paid particular attention to Orthography, a highly specialized subject in the Arab syllabus: this alone was transcendent evidence that he was unique in his century and the portent of the age. Unique or not, he succeeded in selling a girl to the first sovereign of the tiny independent realm of Sahla, south of Zaragoza, a Berber who spent several fortunes on talented singing-girls and musicians. This one, whose name is not recorded, cost ibn Razin three thousand *dinars*, but seems to have been worth every bit of it: besides grace and vivacity, a good figure, a soft voice allied with perfect delivery and pureness of diction, she

---

[1] Abd al-Rahman II broke the record for large families in a prolific dynasty; the founder Abd al-Rahman I had eleven sons and nine daughters: Hisham six sons and five daughters: Hakam I nineteen sons and twenty-one daughters: Abd al-Rahman II forty-five sons and forty-two daughters, an all-time high: Muhammad thirty-three sons and twenty-one daughters: Mundhir only five sons and eight daughters: Abdallah eleven sons and thirteen daughters. No statistics survive of the contribution of the great Abd al-Rahman III, the Victorious, or his son Hakam II.

had the most refined culture, and an unsurpassed command of medicine, natural science and anatomy. A less austere accomplishment was an ability to dance the sabre dance and juggle with edged swords and daggers. Of such talented performers were composed the troupes that the princelings maintained for their private entertainment.

When a good slave fetched such prices, it was inevitable that dishonest persons should lie in wait for the unwary rich, and relieve them of some of their superfluity. The mechanics of the fraud are set out by al-Sakati in the manual he wrote at the beginning of the 12th century for the guidance of the market police, based on a report from the inspector of the slave market at Malaga. Here, it seems, dealers kept intelligent and attractive women who could speak the Romance vernacular and dress themselves after the manner of Christian women. When a customer from some other city comes to the market and asks for a slave from the Christian countries, the dealer first of all replies that for the moment he has none in stock, but is hourly awaiting a consignment, so keeping the customer in a fever of expectation. At last he presents a girl, who feigns to be weary from the journey: an accomplice acting the part of the owner affirms that he bought her at a great price in the Upper Marches, but was well content to pay it for so perfect a jewel. The sale being concluded, the two men and the girl divide the profits, and she goes off with her new master. If she finds him to her taste, she prevails on him to free and wed her: if not, she goes to the police and exhibits identity papers proving beyond cavil that she is a Muslim and a free woman. When the dupe demands reimbursement from the dealer, he answers that the vendor was a well-known importer of Christian slaves, but has left for his own country. *Caveat emptor.*

Al-Sakati tells another cautionary tale about a Granada man who after much experience of women of Andalus swore never to take one to wife. He went all the way to Cordoba, the seat of sovereignty and the metropolis of learning, where the slave market was particularly well stocked, and there bought a girl divinely fair, attired in a robe of silk from the palace looms, such as are worn by the daughters of the Christian princes, and speaking no Arabic. He mounted her on a mule, covering the saddle with a carpet of brocade, and set out for Granada, a servant leading the mule. All the way she expressed delight and wonder at the beauty and strangeness of the countryside, so that his breast was enlarged with delight. When they came to Granada, being unwilling to bring her home by daylight he

lodged her till nightfall in a little house that he owned outside
the city, and then hurried ahead on foot, so as to make all ready
for her arrival.   Now it so happened that outside the gate of the
city there lived a maker of bird-cages, who in his youth had
been a notorious evil-liver, but had now repented, and used to
stay late at work in his shop or by moonlight outside it.   "As
she passed, the old habit of joking with him drove her to say in
Arabic, 'What, that old rake, still alive?' and the man looking
up and seeing her replied, 'You, is it?   Have you returned?'
All of which hearing the astonished slave hastened to relate to
his master."   He after lamenting his misfortune sent a friend
to interrogate the cage-maker, who assured him that the lady
was indeed a trollop and an associate of sinners, whereupon
he became deeply afflicted, and puzzled how he might be rid of
her.   She, however, out of kindness of heart, "divining his
intentions and knowing his licentious customs" (otherwise
perhaps she would not have dared to advise him?), "told him
not to be tormented, but to take her to Almeria, where he could
sell her for more than he had paid.   At that time Almeria was
the chief port of Andalusia and filled with rich merchants.   So
he did: she kept her dress and continued to play her rôle, and
he sold her at a profit."   The moral is what you please.

The royal palaces contained a fantastic population of slaves.
Arabic statistics are always a little fanciful, even when they
affect the most scrupulous accuracy, so that one need not rely
too much on the record of the establishment of Abd al-Rahman
III the Victorious, quoted by al-Maqqari.   He says that there
were 13,750 male servants, each drawing a daily ration of a
pound of meat, and 6,314 females.   Besides these, there were
3,750 Slavonians, drawing four pounds of meat, "but some say
3,787".   This would be the pretorian guard which successive
sovereigns increasingly relied on, till Mansur reorganized the
army on a professional and mercenary basis.   Bread to feed the
fish in the stews reached the surprising daily figure of twelve
thousand loaves, "or perhaps eight hundred".   Another
chronicle assesses male slaves at three thousand and females at
six thousand.   There is little point in trying to reconcile these
figures: they are not utterly incredible, if it is kept in mind that
Abd al-Rahman III lodged the entire administration of the
Empire within the palace precincts of al-Zahra, which was a
mile long and half a mile wide.   Even so, they outclass the
Seraglio of Abdul Hamid at Istanbul: the most spacious estimates of the staff of the Abode of Felicity never went beyond a
thousand women and as many eunuchs.

The extensive domestic staff of the Umayyads was marshalled under the Big Two—*al-fatayan al-kabiran*. They controlled the heads of departments—the commander of the personal bodyguard of the sovereign, the Master of the Kitchen, the Master of Building, the Master of the Horse, the Postmaster, the Falconer, the Jeweller and the Master of the Looms. These last wove a unique tissue for the robes of honour bestowed on ambassadors or guests: they were made of brocade, with inscriptions and portraits of sultans, and fetched fabulous prices whenever they came on the market.

Eunuchs were a relatively late arrival in Cordoba: the first are said to have been a present from the Counts of Barcelona and Tarragona: there were a score of them, and their first employment was in the women's apartments. Once ensconced in the palace, there were no limits to the opportunities of an intelligent man: they were exempt from the sovereign's jealous suspicion, which so often cut short a promising career. The state of an eunuch was no serious disability, once he recovered from the operation; they made good soldiers and magnificent horsemen, with exceptional powers of endurance: history recalls eunuch generals and admirals and governors of provinces both in Byzantium and Islam. (It is odd how often Arab authors refer to the eunuchs' fondness for singing birds.)

They were mostly Slavs from the vast steppes that stretch from Bulgaria to Tashkent: those that reached Spain had been captured by the Germans and sold to Jewish traders in Magdeburg or Verdun, marched down to the sea, paying customs dues to various bishops and potentates on their way, and shipped to Pechina, the now dead sea-port behind Almeria. From there they went to Lucena, north of Malaga, at that time, like Granada later, a Jewish city, where the experts adapted them for their future employment. It was a delicate operation, and the mortality was high, so that a sound eunuch was from four to ten times as expensive as an ordinary slave.

Eunuchs were by no means a Muslim invention. They had been manufactured in the East from time immemorial, and came to the Arabs via Byzantium. Islam categorically prohibited the practice of castration, though Muslims condoned it by buying eunuchs, while leaving the operation to Jews and Christians. The latter had no prejudices: there was even a fanatic sect (the Valesii) that practised self-mutilation to the glory of God, until St. Augustine rebuked them.

The influence of the Slav eunuchs in the palace grew steadily. When Abd al-Rahman II died suddenly in A.D. 852, the senior eunuch called a full meeting of all those, great and small, who held office, convinced them of the advantage of putting Muhammad on the throne instead of his dissipated elder brother Abdallah, the son of Abd al-Rahman's favourite, Tarub.   He then brought Muhammad, disguised as a woman and too terrified to speak, past the terraces where the rightful heir was carousing, as far as the palace door, where the porter refused to admit him until he had seen with his own eyes that Abd al-Rahman was indeed dead.

The eunuchs never looked back as long as the Caliphate lasted: they formed a close corporation, usually called *al-Saqaliba*, the Slavs, which was encouraged by successive sovereigns as a counterpoise to Arabs and Berbers.   When the Caliphate tottered, after Mansur and his son, they were at the bottom of the revolt that brought Sanchol down and delivered Cordoba to fire and the sword.   But their strength was disruptive and not creative: they could exert internal stresses within an existing political structure, but could not build one that stood alone.   When the Empire finally fell to pieces, they tried to play off Berber pretensions against the quasi-national sentiment of the native Andalusians, but the tide was running too strongly, and among the many *Taifas* into which the country split, there were many Arab and many Berber, but only one Slav, at Denia.

.   .   .   .   .

The slave trade was highly organized.   The handiest source was prisoners of war, who were the personal property of the victor; he was entitled to ransom, slaughter or sell them at his absolute discretion.   This was so much a matter of course that in the countless stories true or invented that derive from the traffic there is rarely a word of reprobation for the warrior who exercises his right, although the captives' claim to sympathy is frequently stressed.   One story in which the narrator's disapproval is evident concerns two old *shaykhs*, who are disposed of at a price that is deliberately offensive: but it is not the selling into slavery that is called in question so much as the discourteous manner in which it is conducted.[1]   Sometimes of course the

---

[1] This incident had a political background; the conquering Arabs imported their home feuds into Spain.   A Syrian chieftain, Thalaba ibn Salama, having defeated a combination of Medina and Spanish Arabs sold wives and children to his troops, and put up two venerable Shaykhs of Medina at a sort of Dutch auction, in which succeeding bids had to be lower instead of higher.   They were disposed of one for a dog and the other for a kid.   This would be about A.D. 750.

prisoners were worth next to nothing: at the end of the Cid's eighteen months' blockade of Valencia, the emaciated refugees were sold in the Alcudia market for a loaf of bread or a jar of wine; and evidently, when prisoners were numerous, the market value declined.   There is a charming account in the 13th-century *Canticos de los Moros*, where "our famous Martin Dominguez", who had already been obliged to carry his companions' heads, was brought into the market, and a Moor, a grocer, bought him for thirteen *maravedis*, and sold him to one Mahomet for fifteen.   "And Martin Dominguez said to them, 'Dogs, why do ye handle me thus?   I am worth more than an ass: buy me for twenty *maravedis*.'   And there came Mahomet, another shopkeeper, and bought him for twenty-five *maravedis*."   A gentlemanly proceeding, that certainly comforted our Martin, and augured well for their future relations.

Enterprising dealers often followed the annual campaigns, with the object of buying up prisoners for the slave-market: in this way Jews crowded to the battle of Alarcos.   Their international ramifications made it indifferent who won the victory: Christians could be sold in Cordoba and Muslims in Toledo. This source was supplemented by pirates and traders, who imported shiploads from Egypt and North Africa, Berbers for farm labour, Sudanese for fighting men, Rumis for mariners, men from the Guineas for both.   How little considerations of religion affected the traffic is shown by a typical transaction recorded by Simonet: Christian slave-dealers hire Muslim raiders to kidnap Portuguese Christians at Coimbra, and market them no further away than Santarem.

It was not a squeamish age, and at any rate they stopped short of selling their own kin, which was the practice in the great slave-market of Kaffa in the Crimea.   Here the Castilian ambassador Pedro Tafur saw "fathers sell children and brother brother.   They say the selling of children is no sin, for they are a fruit given by God to use for profit."   The Sultan of Egypt had a permanent agent there for the purchase of Mamelukes, and the Christian dealers (there was a strong Genoese colony there with a Bishop) had a bull from the Pope to buy and keep as slaves Christians of other nations, on the somewhat specious pretext of preventing them from falling into the hands of the infidel and renouncing their faith.   Pedro himself bought two female and one male slave, whom he kept in Cordoba with their offspring.   At Kaffa slaves for sale were kept naked under a cloak of felt, and when a price was named, the cloak was thrown off, and they were made to show their paces, so that any physical defect should be revealed. If a slave died of plague within sixty days of the sale, the buyer got his money back. Tartars fetched a thirty per cent premium on account of their unswerving loyalty: "no Tartar ever betrayed his master".

Not all slaves had kind masters: there was a vast difference between the lot of the town and the country slave. The latter was regarded as cattle: if he was treated humanely, it was because an intelligent master thought it profitable to maintain his labour potential. He was often chained, and stabled for the night in underground cellars from which escape was impossible. Cisterns or bottle-necked silos were particularly adapted to that end: there is one in good repair in the Alcazaba at Malaga, where Christians were accommodated, and at Granada, between the Alcazaba and Carlos V's preposterous palace, the Plaza de los Algibes has a suite of them. During the hours of daylight the work demanded of them was exhausting: anyone who has visited Ronda will sympathize with the Christian prisoners who spent their days carrying waterskins from the bottom of the Tajo up the interminable steps to their masters' kitchens.

The situation of an urban slave was far from hopeless: the rights of female slaves were clearly laid down by the Shari'a law. Any concubine who gave birth to a son at once became a person of importance—*umm walad*—and usually another centre of intrigue. She and her son had a claim to maintenance that could be enforced by process of law: at the death of her owner she was emancipated. The problem of dealing with his predecessor's women-folk that faced a new sovereign was not infrequently solved by his leaving the whole establishment intact *in statu quo*, and building himself a new palace.

A female slave was not entirely a helpless chattel: a man could sell or give her away, but could not apparently force her into his bed if she was unwilling. He certainly had every means of making her life uncomfortable, and it was probably infrequent that a slave was recalcitrant, as all her prospects of a successful career depended on pleasing her master. There are however such cases on record: a sad story is told of a lovely and accomplished slave who was bought up with the whole establishment on the death of her master; she was so attached to his memory that she refused to bed with her new master, and even preferred menial service to entertaining him with her singing. Such cases were doubtless as rare then as they would be now: it requires a very special temperament to remain inflexible when compliance offers so great a reward: one is driven to the conclusion that the new owner was an impossible *parvenu*.

For there were literally no limits to what could be achieved by an able concubine: history is full of examples; perhaps the most striking is the story of the fabulous palace of al-Zahra built by Abd al-Rahman III. The beginning of it was the fortune bequeathed by a favourite for the pious object of ransoming Muslim captives. For many years the Caliph's arms had been so consistently victorious that no appreciable number of Muslim captives was to be found, and the disposal of the legacy presented a problem that was solved only by the suggestion of another favourite that he should build a new palace and give it her name.

The Caliphate of Cordoba gave women, slave or free, a far greater measure of freedom than Turkey before Ataturk, or Syria up to a few years ago. I can remember when the charming daughters of Bedi' beg al-Mu'ayyad, encouraged by the liberty not so much granted as imposed on Turkish women, announced their intention of walking unveiled in the streets of Damascus, but were deterred by the threat that if they did they would be beaten and their faces sprayed with vitriol. In Cordoba a thousand years earlier it is clear from various narratives that women could walk about unveiled and join in social functions where men were invited. One has only to read the story of the poet Ramadi's *coup de foudre* or ibn Hazm's tender account of his youthful passion for a slave in his father's house: and there are many other tales that prove how much independence they enjoyed.

There is indeed much evidence of an abiding attachment between master and slave: one curious indication is furnished by a group of tombstones with Kufic inscriptions which recently came to light at Cordoba. They commemorate concubines— *jariyat*: the formula employed recalls not their social virtues but the fact that they died in the full faith of Islam, and if God wills shall be raised in it again. There follows a prayer to Allah to yield assent to the intercession of the Prophet, and the date of the death in precise detail. Though such an inscription may seem to a Christian of to-day no more than an empty formality, it is no slight tribute in a Muslim country, where the doctrine of surrender prescribes that the dead should be tipped into the grave with scant ceremony, and the mourner quit his mourning when he turns his back on the cemetery.

There are many other memorials of attachment to slaves:

it is related of a 10th century Caliph in Bagdad that he was so grieved by the death of his favourite eunuch Ziraq, that he could not endure to live in his palace, where everything reminded him of his loss, and so moved to other quarters; for less obvious reasons he also poured four hundred jars of old wine into the Tigris.   Less extravagant but certainly no less sincere was the devotion of one Khalaf, a freedman who in 1009 was implicated in a rising against Mansur in favour of the shadow-Caliph Hisham.   He made good his escape, but could not bear separation from a certain slave, and returned to fetch her away.   He was discovered and taken.   Ibn Hazm writes of his end, "I remember seeing him crucified in the meadow by the Guadalquivir: he had so many javelins in him that he looked like a hedgehog."

CHAPTER EIGHT

LOVE

THE POSITION of women under the Caliphate was very much the same as in other Muslim countries at other times, except that seclusion seems to have been a good deal less strict. So much depended on the personal views of the sovereign, and on the degree of deference he owed to the Maliki *faqihs*: these fought an up and down battle against the easy-going tolerance that came natural to the Umayyads, and not infrequently succeeded in imposing their ruthless bigotry on the lighter-hearted Andalusians. In spite of their efforts, however, there were long periods during which women enjoyed a large measure of emancipation, and by and large they were more accessible than was till lately usual in most Muslim countries.

The ultimate sanctions were not revoked: for while certain princesses were gratified by love poems addressed to them, their male relatives were always apt to take a different view. The Mughit family, great aristocrats that had frequently held high office at Cordoba, was utterly ruined because one of its scions composed an ardent ode to a Caliph's daughter; and on another occasion, a slave-girl, whom Mansur was thinking of buying, made the mistake of singing a love poem addressed to his Queen and mistress, Aurora the Basque—a lack of vision that cost her her life. And how often have workmen excavating on Muslim sites come on bones beneath their living-room floors.

There has never been a time when women were not the subject of disagreement between doctors and sages. Their utter perversity has been an article of faith with many creeds, including our own. The Indian law-giver, Manu, laid down fourteen centuries before the Christian era that any woman should be adjudged an adulteress, if she had been alone with a man the time it takes to cook an egg. In the 11th century, the philosopher al-Ghazali, who was greatly drawn to the Almoravid reforming movement, held a very low opinion of women; gardens where anyone could pluck a fruit, saddles that anyone might bestride. Less trenchant moralists still thought of them as pearls that it was wiser to keep in a casket: wherefore the mad Caliph Hakim in Cairo forbade the making of women's shoes, to keep them virtuously within doors. Men who remembered their childhood spent in the sickly warmth of the harem carried into their mature years an indelible distrust of women; ibn Hazm writes that he was so deeply versed in their mysteries that he conceived a violent antipathy for them and the worst possible opinion. He acknowledged that they taught him the Quran and much verse, and perhaps laid the foundations of his literary style, but recalling no less their caresses and above all what they told him about one another, he sets them down as devoid of any but sexual thoughts, and interested in nothing but the various forms of venery: nor in fact, says he, were they made for anything else. Men have other cares: they are kept busy with earning money and making a career, in study, travel, hunting, war, official charges, in crushing rebellions and tilling the soil; they have less time for such nonsense.

A century later, the great Averroes is moved to compassion for the misery of womankind, created for nothing but childbearing and suckling, and so reduced to a servitude that has destroyed all capacity for higher pursuits. He is saddened by their lack of moral faculties: they live like plants, looking after their menfolk: hence the misery that devours the cities, since there are twice as many women as men, and they have no means of earning their sustenance.

His tenderness led him into an overstatement: in Muslim countries the poor are rarely left to starve; but financial independence was a goal not easy of attainment. The chief liberal profession open to women was that of copyist: hundreds of them supported themselves (and perhaps their husbands) by copying the Quran; at one time there were as many as a hundred and seventy women so occupied in one quarter of Cordoba. History has preserved the name of one, Fatima, an ancient dame who wrote exquisitely and died a virgin.

A few blue-stockings comet across the firmament: in the 11th century there was Wallada, a daughter of one of the fleeting caliphs of the *fitna*, who led a completely unconstrained life under the *Taifas*, keeping a *salon* and carrying on affairs with poets. She was a poet herself: she had a *grande passion* for another poetess, Muhja, which she enshrined in ecstatic verse. Her liaison with the poet ibn Zaydun stimulated the literary production of both of them: when she tired of him, she gave him his *congé* in some pretty gross verses. Muhja also could be direct in declining the advances of members of the *cénacle*.

Other women less renowned were very likely more delicate: it is however the opinion of Pérès, an authority on Andaluz poetry with whom no sensible man would presume to differ,

that what little verse the poetesses left contains strong evidence
that they enjoyed such freedom: they show an initiative and
resolution that do not flower in a stale seraglio.   The dawning
cult of *amor cortes* may have something to do with it, but the
women's contribution to literature could only spring from
independence.

The measure of this liberty can be reckoned by a story told
by ibn Hazm in his *Ars Amatoria*, the Neck of the Dove, in the
chapter on love at first sight.   The poet, Yusuf ibn Harun,
commonly called al Ramadi,[1] was passing through the Gate of
the Druggists at Cordoba, where the women were wont to
gather, when he saw a girl who "captured" in his phrase "the
cockles of his heart, and love for her permeated all the members
of his body".   He was on his way to the Mosque, but turned
aside to follow her; she made for the bridge and crossed it on
her way to the suburb on the other side, known as the Arrabal.
As she passed the gardens of the Banu Marwan, (may God have
absolved them!), where the royal house had their tombs, the
girl saw that he was following her and stopped to ask him what
he wanted.   He set out at length the torment that was consuming him on account of her charms: "put these things from
you", she said, "and seek not my ruin; you can not come by
your desire."   "I am content to gaze on you," he said, and she
answered, "That you may."   Then he asked her, "Lady mine,
are you free or a slave?"   "A slave."   "And what is your
name?"   "Khalwa."   "And who is your master?"   "By
God, sooner shall you learn what is in the seventh heaven."
She made to go, but he asked her, "Oh lady mine, when shall I
see you again?"   "Where you saw me, at the same hour, every
Friday.   And now will you go first, or shall I?"   He answered,
"Go you first, with the protection of God," and she went towards the bridge, and he could not follow her, because she kept
on looking round.   When she had passed the Gate of the
Bridge, he ran after her, but could not come up with her.   And
al-Ramadi says, "From that moment till now, I do not stir from
the Gate of the Druggists and the Arrabal, but never had news
of her, and know not whether the earth or the sky swallowed her
up: but my heart is aflame for her."

There is alas! another version of the story, ascribed to the
poet himself, told with less art and probably more truth, which
shows him in a less attractive light.   In this account, he finds

---

[1] The Arabic form of his sobriquet *abu Ceniza*, which means the father of
ashes: but the explanation of the nickname is lost: perhaps a platinum
blond, always admired under the Umayyads.

out that the girl's price would be three hundred *dinars*—a very reasonable figure—and admits without a blush that by putting her into a panegyric which had been commissioned by the Governor of Zaragoza, he so worked on that simple soldier's feelings that he increased Ramadi's honorarium by so much; but when he met her again, he decided to keep the cash.

In neither version is there the faintest suggestion of a stolen interview, or indeed of anything unusual in meeting the girl unveiled; and there are plenty of other passages in the literature of the Caliphate that bear witness to the freedom of movement of women in the cities of Andalus. In "The Thousand and One Nights", where the scene is laid in Bagdad, there are plenty of meetings between young gallants and slaves, but they are always illicit and spiced with danger. In Cordoba no surprise is felt when slave girls communicate freely with guests of their master; they mix without restraint in social gatherings, and if we may trust ibn Hazm, steal kisses under the noses of the assembly. He has a story of a youth and a slave who were in love, and used to sit on the same couch, with a large cushion between them, such as was offered to Very Important Persons. They used to stretch out under a somewhat flimsy pretext of fatigue, and kiss behind it. This seems an extreme instance, but there are many other references to parties where the sexes mingled as freely as in Bloomsbury; as for example in the more edifying story of another young man who was in love with a slave and made improper proposals to her. She reprimands him: "By God, I shall have to quarrel with you in public, and before everyone." A few days later there is a party "with the great magnates and the most eminent men of the Caliphate, together with a multitude of people of standing, women and relatives", the young man being one of the last. When it is her turn, the slave sings:

> "A youth, lovely as a gazelle, or the full moon,
>   Or the sun when it opens a path through the clouds,
>   Captured my heart with his languorous glances
>   And his waist like a branch for slimness.
>   I humbled myself before him as a docile lover;
>   I subjected myself, as one madly enamoured;
>   But come to me, my Love, in a lawful manner,
>   For I like not union by forbidden paths."

There was the same freedom in the lecture-room: women had opportunities of study and not infrequently set up as lecturers themselves, in such subjects as jurisprudence and the interpretation of the Quran. Ribera mentions a famous school founded by one Karima in the heart of Mecca, where many scions of noble Spanish families went to complete their studies; while in Andalusia there were several schools open to both sexes: a girl could attend lectures with her father, or a wife with her husband. Women followed public classes, and at the conclusion of the course received the same diploma which qualified them for posts in the ministries. They could then either open schools of their own or, more frequently, teach in one conducted by their parents: there was a family affair of this kind at Cordoba, kept by the Banu Hazm, at which the father taught the children, the son the adults, and the daughter the girls. Brilliant studies might in very rare instances win far greater prizes: there was Lubna, who became librarian and secretary to Hakam II; and it is told of one Umayyad prince, that he was so struck by the intellectual attainments of a Nubian slave, who had sat at the feet of Malik, that he married her, black skin and all.

These however were very exceptional cases: the most promising field for women was still the harem, as wife or concubine, and the best education was one that taught them to exploit their charms.

Unfortunately the market was against them: they had not only to outshine their sisters, but also to overcome unfair competition from another quarter. Surfeit in the harem produced two widely divergent reactions, on the one hand the *amour courtois* that was later to inspire the chivalry of Christian Europe, and on the other homosexuality.

The men of Andalus had no prejudice against relations with either sex, but seem to have regarded sodomy as the more spiritual of the two. The stereotyped enumeration of female charms which is the stock-in-trade of every ardent versifier gives a clear idea of what they most prized; the inescapable slender waist springing from wide hips, the antelope's neck and gazelle's eyes, the slow swimming gait, as if she walked on eggs: some poets even compare their loves with wild cows. The poet-prince Mu'tamid writes in a lyric burst of reminiscence, "How many nights have I spent sporting in the shade with women of opulent hips and tenuous waist." (His liking for opulent figures is shared by the present-day Andalusian.) But very little else was expected of a woman, and even those charms were not her monopoly.[1]

[1] Ibn Muqana, a poet of the 11th century, sings of his beloved that the branch of his waist curves from the sandhills of his hips, and the night of his hair rises over the clear dawn of his face."

I

The woman's contribution to love was entirely passive, and not diversified by any accidents of a spiritual or even mental content. Even such qualities as loyalty were not expected from the Beloved; of the lover, yes: he must remain loyal even when betrayed; but in the passive object of his cult, loyalty was praiseworthy, if it existed, but in no wise obligatory. The higher love was deemed a prerogative of the male sex; consequently a poet sees nothing strange in dedicating to a man the following exquisite sentiments:

> I love thee with a love that knows not change,
> While so many human loves are only mirage;
> I consecrate to thee a love pure and unspotted;
> In my heart thy affection is written plain to see;
> If my spirit held aught beside thee,
> I would tear it out and rend it with my hands.
> I desire of thee nothing but love,
> Beyond love I ask for nothing:
> If I attain it, I count the whole world and mankind
> No more than specks of dust and insects.

In the other scale one may put the verses of another contemporary poet, the Prince of the Amnesty,[1] dedicated to his cousin Hatiba, whom he wished to marry:

> I stipulated in the marriage contract that I would serve her as a slave,
> And I have conveyed my soul to her as a marriage portion,
> I have given her my realm, my mind, my life and my soul:
> And nothing is more precious than the soul.

The notarial metaphors that for us detract from the beauty of the lyric are in Arab eyes a delicate *tour de force*: the sentiment itself would be hard to parallel in European poetry of the 12th

---

[1] This great-grandson of Abd al-Rahman III al-Nasir, who was himself Caliph for a moment in 1023, had a romantic life divided into three equal parts: at the age of sixteen he killed his father, who was his rival in the affections of a young lady; he spent the next sixteen years in prison, and was then pardoned by Mansur at the instance of a pet ostrich. The dictator had retired to the peace of his garden with an armful of petitions, which he found too numerous to study, so he crumpled them one by one and tossed them to a young ostrich, which he had brought up from the egg. The bird swallowed them, all but one, which he brought back to his master; Mansur crumpled it tighter, but the ostrich again rejected it and laid it in his lap. Mansur then acknowledged the mandate of Allah, read the petition and released the prisoner, who was thenceforth known as al-Mustadhir, the Pardoned. He counts as a leading poet, and is the subject of a delightful study by Emilio Garcia Gomez.

century. It is anything but unique in contemporary Andalusian poetry; the love of a man for a maid is constantly expressed with the same tenderness and apparent sincerity, and
the anthologists tell stories of devotion that carry conviction.
There is the tale of the freedman Khalaf implicated in an
unsuccessful revolt, who, after making good his escape, went
back and lost his life in trying to save his beloved. There is
the heartrending tale of the lover who went to say good-bye
to his beloved, but found that she had already gone, and so died
of a broken heart. There is above all ibn Hazm's enchanting
tale of the two men captive of the charms of the same slave,
which deserves a place in any anthology.

A man of al-Andalus lost his fortune, and sold a slave to whom
he was deeply attached, never thinking that his soul would
strain after her, as it came to pass; for when the slave was in the
hands of the purchaser, his heart came near to breaking, and he
offered him all his remaining goods and even his liberty in
return for the girl, but the man refused. His neighbours
interceded for him, but in vain. At last, beside himself with
grief, he went to the Sultan, who was sitting in a high chamber,
from which he overlooked all the town. He told his tale
humbly and asked for help: the Sultan was touched and
summoned the new owner, and said, "Here is a stranger,
whose story you know; he has asked me to speak for him."
But the man answered that he loved the girl even more than
the other, and if he gave her up, he would be at the Sultan's
feet on the morrow, in even worse case. The Sultan and those
about him sought to convince him, offering him a great part of
their fortunes, but he ever refused on account of the great love
he bore her. Then the Sultan turned to the petitioner and
said, "Thou hast witnessed. I can do no more: the man loves
her more than thou, and fears to be in worse distress if he gives
her up. Resign thyself therefore to what God has ordained."
Then said the man of Andalus, "Canst thou do no more?" and
the Sultan answered, "Is there more to do than to supplicate
and offer money? I can do no more." When he heard this,
he joined hands and feet together, and threw himself down
from the window of that chamber. The Sultan was shocked
and called for his pages, and the pages ran down and picked
him up; but God had ordained that he should not suffer any
grievous hurt. When therefore he returned to the presence, the
Sultan asked, "Why didst thou so?" and he answered, "Oh
King, because I cannot live without her." Then said the
Sultan, "God is great: here is the manner of determining

this matter." Then he turned to the other, and said, "Oh
thou! Thou hast said that thou lovest this woman more than
he and fearest to be in worse case than he." And he answered,
"Thus it is." Then said the King, "Thy adversary has shown
a clear proof of his love, throwing himself down in search of
death, but God Honoured and Powerful watched over him.
Do thou now show proof of thy love in throwing thyself from
this window, as did thy adversary. If thou diest, it will be that
thy hour has struck; but if not, thou wilt have a surer claim to
the slave, and thy adversary will leave thee in peace. But if
thou wilt not, I will take her from thee by force and give her to
him." The man hesitated for a while, and then said, "I will
throw myself down," but when he came to the window and saw
the void beneath him, he drew back. Then said the King, "By
God I will do as I said." The man again made to throw himself down, and again drew back. Then said the King, seeing
him unwilling, "Thou shalt not play with us. Ho pages! seize
him and throw him from the window." When the man saw
the sure intent of the King, he said, "Oh King, my heart is
reconciled to the loss of my slave." The King answered, "God
will reward thee," and bought the slave and gave her to the
man who had sold her. Then the two went away.

The inflammable temperament of the men of Andalus led
them frequently to extremities which seem incredible: to go
mad or die for love is commonplace. The Amir Abd
al-Rahman II, campaigning in the north of his dominions,
dreamt of his favourite, Tarub, and hastily appointing a
general to carry on with the war, rode back post haste to Cordoba. And there was a *faqih* with a great reputation, a scholar
whose mature intelligence should have kept him out of danger;
he was in Bagdad, looking for the house of a colleague who had
invited him to a meal, and losing his way in the intricate maze
of streets, strayed into a blind alley. At the end of it was a girl,
unveiled, who called out to him, "Oh thou! this street has no
issue." The one sight of the girl was fatal: he fell instantly
and utterly in love, and being a man of principles left Bagdad
for Basra to escape temptation, and there died of his hopeless
passion.

They could make fools of themselves, too, even the most
eminent. One Sa'id, a theologian and son of the famous
Mundhir ibn Sa'id, who was Qadi of Cordoba and led the
prayers in the Great Mosque, was so enamoured of a slave of
his that he offered to free her and take her to wife. She pre-
tended to agree, only stipulating that he should shorten his

luxuriant beard. The old dotard committed this iniquity, (a
Muslim having once decided what hair he will leave on his face
is expected to adhere to his decision), and then summoned
witnesses to the formal emancipation of the slave, who so soon as
she was free refused to marry him. His brother Hakam aggravated his humiliation by himself marrying the girl—incredible
behaviour on the part of the chief of the free-thinking Mu'tazilis,
a man distinguished for his piety, an ascetic and a poet. The
poet clearly got the better of the ascetic.

It is difficult at many hundred years' remove to arrive at any
reliable appraisement of love in Andalus: the only elements of
judgment to hand are literary, either stories of lovers whose
cases would not have been thought worth recording if they
had not been exceptional, or poems addressed to the beloved;
and Arab poets were notoriously insincere. There must have
been a great number of families living in tranquil obscurity,
whose decent domestic routine attracted neither the jealousy of
the Fates nor the interest of the historians. A wife was by no
means a chattel: the *shari'a* law, which regarded marriage not
as a sacrament but a civil contract, fortified her position when
her charms began to fade; and it is a fair assumption that most
families jogged along at least as well as the *mariages de convenance*
of recent years, and provided as little matter for lyrical comment. The poets found their material in the exceptional, and
it is clear from the mass of verse that survives that the correct
lover of the day had to endure not only the suffering imposed
by separation and other circumstances beyond his control, but
also every kind of torment and humiliation inflicted in cold
blood by the cruel fair, all of which he must endure without
contumacy, while conscientiously pining away, and in really
memorable cases actually dying.

The Elizabethans had something like it, with their tongues
in their cheeks, but the last half-century, with its Teutonic
preoccupation with sexual perversions, has nothing but contempt for this attitude, and has awarded it the nasty label of
masochism; but there is no compelling reason why it should
not be given credit for a foundation of decent sentiment, even if
it was touched off by a hangover from indulgence. Two
schools of thought coincide in deriving it from the harem system,
the one thinking of the proprietor sickened by excess of opportunity, the other of the unauthorized aspirant frustrated by
excess of impediment. However that may be, there is no
question that under a variety of names, chaste love or *amor
cortes* became very fashionable in Andalus, and it is strongly

affirmed by some scholars and as strongly denied by others, that it is in Muslim Spain that one must look for the origin of *amour courtois*, knight errantry and the Provençal courts of love, that betokened a respect for women quite new in the savagery of contemporary Christendom.

This timid and self-effacing worship of an unattainable she was not born in al-Andalus, but imported from Bagdad. It was the creation of the poet Muhammad ibn Da'ud al-Isfahani, who had himself borrowed the conception from Plato. Ibn Da'ud, whose Persian extraction predisposed him to a mystical philosophy, was born in the second half of the 9th century; as a boy he suffered from a sensibility and diffidence that earned him the nickname of '*usfur al-shawq*, the little bird that hides in the thorns. His precocity was extreme: he was lecturing on jurisprudence by the time he was sixteen, and throughout his short life he took an active part in metaphysical discussion, and composed a number of treatises before dying at the age of forty. The mainspring of his life, to quote Emilio Garcia Gomez, was a lasting and hopeless passion he conceived for one of his schoolfellows, which he dominated but could not quite eradicate. The compulsion he felt to reconcile with the teaching of his faith a passion that he judged illicit led him to work out his system. Starting from the Platonic conception of love as a form of madness inflicted by the gods, unpredictable, irrational and inescapable, he devises a course of conduct based on the pre-Islamic legend of the Banu Udra, the sons of virginity, who were an Arab tribe celebrated by the poets for their genius for unrequited love, from which they suffered in a superlative degree and even died of its effects.[1]

This elevated ideal, to which perhaps the celibates of the Thebaid made some contribution, became so fashionable in Bagdad that its adepts fabricated a tradition that the Prophet had said, "Whoso loves and keeps chaste and dies, dies a martyr."

Plato also provided him with a theory of predestined affinities, sister souls who go seeking one another all their lives, sometimes meeting and so attaining felicity. This he found in the "Banquet", in the fairy-tale produced by Aristophanes to explain the longing for perfection of an imperfect creature. In the beginning they were one whole—ibn Da'ud thinks of them as perfect spheres—but became puffed up with pride, till Zeus clove them in two, and ever after the two halves seek reunion. A little of ibn Da'ud's theory has survived till to-day in Spain,

[1] They were apparently Christians: see Alfred Guillaume: "Islam."

where the curious expression *"media naranja"* (half orange) means one's better half. *cava mitad*

Ibn Da'ud expounded his sytem in verse, in the Book of the Flower: with a nice regard for mathematical symmetry typical of the Arab mind, he enshrined his thoughts in one hundred poems each containing, beside the chapter heading, exactly one hundred lines.   Sixty or seventy years later the doctrine was current in Spain, and a well known poet of Jaen, ibn Faraj, enriched the subject by composing an anthology called the Book of the Orchard, in which he outpointed ibn Da'ud by assembling two hundred poems each comprising two hundred lines.   Ibn Hazm certainly knew the original work of ibn Da'ud.

Bagdadi or Udri love had its vogue in the last years of the Caliphate, in aesthetic and aristocratic circles: it was part of the programme of the highly cultured *coterie* that included ibn Hazm and ibn Shuhayd and furnished one of the last Caliphs with a short-lived ministry of all the talents, on the eve of the *débâcle*.   Its appeal was strengthened by a general revolt against the materialism of Islam, which was beginning to manifest itself in the various schools of Sufiism.   One cannot help wondering how far the poets' exquisite protestations of continence corresponded with reality, but there can be no doubt at all about the vogue of the new style of spiritual love.   All was suffering and abnegation and submission; even when the Beloved was forthcoming, the Lover must abstain, so that the pure force of his passion should not be impaired by fulfilment: better death than satiety.   Ibn Faraj boasts, "My beloved desired union, but I turned chastely aside, and Satan did not have his will. . . . My Beloved was for me a garden of lovely sights and sweet perfumes: I am not a brute beast that takes a garden for fodder."   A poet even refuses to meet his Beloved: "My soul when I sleep is with thee, withdrawn from the senses: the union of souls is ten thousand times more estimable than the union of bodies."

The last chapter of ibn Hazm's unique manual of love, the "Neck of the Dove", is a spirited eulogy of chastity, and presages that *amor de lonh* and cult of the *princesse lointaine*, so dear to the troubadours.   "One of the best things a man can do in his loves is to keep chastity, not commit sin or lewdness, nor spurn the reward that his Creator makes ready for him among the delights of the eternal mansion, and not disobey his Lord, who has loaded him with favours, has sent him his prophets and established his word firmly upon him."   There

follows a lively description of the Day of Judgment, when
Gehenna will gape for those who have rebelled and chosen
earthly pleasures, while those who have kept their souls from
stumbling will have Paradise for their dwelling-place. "How
much greater shall be the reward of him that hid in his heart a
hotter flame than embers of tamarind, who has suffered in his
inward parts a laceration keener than the sword and swallowed
draughts bitterer than colocynth!"

The course of true love is traced methodically in the "Neck
of the Dove". It begins with the ways of falling in love,
arranged in ascending order of probability—from dreaming of
her, from hearing her described, from seeing her once, from
longer acquaintance. Ibn Hazm himself cannot really under-
stand any way but the last: he was ever slow to love and never
wearied of his love once given. There are chapters on the
symptoms of love, on verbal allusions, on signalling with the
eyes and correspondence, (he recommends the destruction of
letters), on the *dramatis personae* concerned in every affair of the
heart, the messenger, the friendly helper, the spy, the slanderer:
a lyrical chapter on union with the beloved, which he likens to
plants drinking after a drought, or flowers gleaming after
spring showers, or the murmur of a runlet among flowerbeds,
and proclaims as outrivalling any earthly delight, "the favour
of the Sultan and the privilege of wealth, or being something
after being nothing, or return after long exile, or safety after
fear". All of which he had known in his own body. This
culmination is followed by chapters on more painful subjects,
quarrels, treachery, separation, sickness, forgetfulness and
death; among them is one treating of the unsuccessful lover
and how he makes the best of his misfortune.

No complaints, but gentle resignation: the philosophical
acceptance of half a loaf when more is not to be had; he must
be glad to see her and have his greeting returned. One man
begs his obdurate charmer to make him a promise, even if she
has the firm intention of not keeping it. A surely extreme case
is a man whose beloved had stuck a knife into him; he kissed
the wound and bathed it with his tears; beside this the maiden
who kissed her beloved's footprints in the garden path pales
into the commonplace. Certain poets console themselves with
composing verses in which they profess to be content that they
and their loves tread the same earth beneath the same sky.
They need not be taken too seriously.

So they loved all those centuries ago, with exquisite refinement, writing verses full of elegant conceits, longing to be the

bird that feeds from her hand or the love-letter she will hide in
her bosom, treasuring locks of hair scented with amber and
bedewed with rosewater and wrapped in silk or brocade, or
less poetically exchanging used toothpicks or gum mastic
partially chewed.   They hold solemn courts of love and gravely
debate fine points of amatory law: a lover claims the roses
which his glances had brought to her cheeks, on the ground
that the harvest belongs to the man that sowed it.   There is a
report of a case decided by the doughty blue-stocking Wallada.
"Your glance wounds our hearts, and ours your cheeks:
which of us merits the punishment of exile?"   She delivered
judgment in favour of the woman, on the ground that the
wound in the cheek was plain to see, but the wound in the heart
required to be substantiated by witnesses.

All very refined and courtly and more than a little artificial
and precious: but if one may trust more prosaic observers, this
ethereal attitude was anything but general in Muslim Spain,
and by no means in harmony with the inclinations of the
majority of women.   Ibn Abdun, compiling his rules for the
administration of Seville at the beginning of the 12th century, is
at pains to multiply the precautions that the true believer must
take to protect the virtue of his womenfolk from the enterprises
of lawyers, bachelors, policemen, court ushers and hawkers, and
even the soldiers on the top floor of the barracks overlooking
the cemetery.   Women need also to be protected against their
own frailty: he will not have them wash clothes in the orchards,
which seems to have served as a prelude to less commendable
pursuits: fortune-tellers are to be distrusted, they are all bawds,
and sewing-women all prostitutes.

The ancient calling of procuress never lacked for practitioners
in Andalus, and has provided two immortal figures in Spanish
literature: Dame Trotaconventos in the "Book of True Love"
of the Archpriest of Hita, an author ranking with Chaucer and
Villon, and La Celestina,[1] created by an unknown author at
the beginning of the 16th century.   An earlier poet, Abu Ja'far
Ahmad ibn Sa'id, dedicated a lyric to one of their forerunners,
which I have translated from the version of Garcia Gomez in
his "Poesia Arabigo-andaluza".

The procuress that takes pride in her infamy, better at covering up than
    night to the wayfarer;
She enters every house, and no-one knows how far she makes her way;
Courteous, with a warm welcome for those she meets: her steps do not vex
    the neighbours;

[1] "The Procuress".

Her cloak is never folded away, it is more restless than a battle pennon;

As soon as she knew her usefulness, she learnt the distinction between crime and subtlety.

She knows not where stands the mosque, but is familiar with the taverns,

Always smiling, very pious, and has a fund of jokes and stories;

Has at her finger-ends the science of arithmetic and the craft of making horoscopes and charms;

She cannot buy herself shoes out of her purse, but is rich in the midst of penury:

With the smoothness of her speech she is capable of coupling fire and water.

CHAPTER NINE

FUN AND GAMES

THE MUSLIM in quest of relaxation found his liberty of action seriously curtailed by the interference of puritan *faqihs*— the scribes and pharisees of the time, who far too frequently enforced their protests by appeal to authority. These killjoys could cite Scripture to their purpose: the Quran was too full of passages banning the more agreeable pastimes. Even the most blameless of field sports, if not explicitly prohibited, were frowned on by implication. Had not the Prophet (on him the blessing and the peace!) stated in an accepted *hadith* that the angels attended only three varieties of corporate recreation— horse-racing, shooting at the mark and—of all things—copulation? What then of hunting, hawking, polo, all wholesome and inoffensive pursuits? And as for indoor amusements, while admittedly the abuse of wine might give occasion for censure, surely its use within reason was not a sin? And music and song: surely innocent diversions? Even chess, that fascinating and intellectual game, that allowed the full-blooded warrior to sublimate his combative urges (no doubt the tenth century thought along twentieth century lines, though ignorant of the patter), was it possible that the Prophet so undervalued its therapeutic efficacy as to declare that it was suitable only for those barbarians that grinned at one another when they met, like so many calves?

It is hardly surprising that the pretensions of the *faqihs* came to be disregarded by the majority of good citizens, except when for political reasons the sovereign judged it expedient to conciliate the cloth.

Hunting, in both the English and the American sense, was the privilege of the rich and powerful. Not that the Amirs promulgated jealous and savage laws to prevent poaching, as in feudal England and France, but simply because it called for organization, horses, beaters and so on, which were beyond the means of all but amirs and nobles. Their subjects were not exempt of jealousy, and quite ready to give vent to it on occasion. It is related that after Charlemagne had raided down to Zaragoza, Hisham, the second Amir, had counter-raided, recovered all the country the Franks had occupied, and pushed on as far as Narbonne, bringing back much booty, including forty-five thousand gold *dinars*, which he applied to enlarging the mosque at Cordoba and rebuilding the Roman bridge over the Guadalquivir. His ungrateful subjects then said he had only done so for his own convenience when hunting, so he was obliged to make an oath, and keep it, never again to cross the bridge.

There was a certain amount of riding to hounds, or at least coursing game on horseback: the poets make frequent impassioned references to the great-hearted Salukis, whose nobility won the Muslims to forget their ritual uncleanness, and accord them a place in their homes. More frequently they rode out hawking in the valley of the Guadalquivir, which was alive with pheasant, partridge, pigeon, ringdove and quail, and—most prized of all—cranes. Abd al-Rahman I, the founder of the dynasty, was breaking camp on an expedition against the Christians, when a courtier hastened up with news of a flight of cranes settling near the tents, fully expecting the advance to be deferred while the Amir rode after this choice quarry. Abd al-Rahman however refused to turn aside, but worked off the disappointment which he certainly suffered, by composing a famous poem. "Call me not to hunt cranes," it begins, "I desire only to hunt the infidels, whether they lurk in ambush or on the mountain tops. When the sun at midday darts his flaming rays, my canopy is the shade of the fluttering banner: dearer to me than gardens or tall palaces the desert and life in the tent."

For the most exciting sport of all was war, which at that time was conducted with some respect for the rules. Etiquette required that an emissary should be sent to the enemy camp to agree on a day for the battle; and the proceedings customarily opened with a champion riding out and challenging all comers to single combat. In Spanish he was called Campeador, and the most famous was the Cid, Don Rodrigo Bivar el Campeador. The greatest pains were taken to observe the correct protocol: it was even possible for an enemy champion to be asked to arbitrate on a matter in dispute in one's own ranks. "When Muhalib was about to join battle with certain heretics in Khurasan, a dispute arose in his army, which was the greater poet, of Jabir and Farazdaq. Muhalib refused to pronounce, for fear of drawing on himself (as he said) the hatred of one of the two packs of mad dogs, and advised them to refer the matter to the heretics. The battle therefore being joined, a heretic came out and challenged the believers to combat: the warrior who took up the challenge first asked his opinion regarding the controversy, and he voted for Jabir." Such an incident was possible only in a community which esteemed war and poetry alike pursuits becoming to a gentleman.

There are many references to a game not unlike polo; and it is probable that some form of bull-fighting took place in the Roman amphitheatre at Merida and elsewhere, apparently a duel between the bull and a horseman armed with a lance, like the modern *rejoneador*. It is uncertain whether the Moors introduced the sport or adopted it from Spain: I am told that Strabo has a reference to it somewhere: the Almoravids and Almohads were certainly captivated by Andalusia and adopted many local fashions. They took Spanish bulls back to the Maghrib, and one of their chiefs was unlucky enough to be fatally gored by a Spanish cow in his garden at Marrakesh.

In a milder key, they all had a consuming passion for picnics and garden parties. Any occasion would serve, but best of all were the Muslim or Christian feast-days; the latter if anything were more popular because they followed the Julian calendar, and could be relied on to come round at the same season, whereas the Muslim feasts followed the lunar year and came a month earlier every year and were soon out of season. The Easter picnic, still celebrated all over the Levant by Muslim and Christian alike and probably earlier in origin than either faith, was cordially taken over, with all its apparatus of dyed ggs and barbecued lamb. There were also numerous saints' day pilgrimages, the present-day Greek *panegyri*, where hospitality was offered by the monks; they had the additional attraction that out of deference to one's hosts, one could not decently refuse the proffered wine. Certain monasteries offered the most lavish hospitality, like the Church of the Crows in Algarbe, already famous in the 12th century. This was the shrine of Saint Vincent at Sagres, where Cape Saint Vincent lunges out into the Atlantic. It was splendidly endowed with both lands and the gifts of pilgrims; and Idrisi, the geographer, tells of the custom which obtained from the highest antiquity: "whoso visited the church might nowise leave until he had tasted of the hospitality of the monks. Moreover there are always ten crows on the dome, neither more nor less, nor has anyone ever seen one of them absent". Legend says that Saint Vincent's body was buried there after martyrdom, and his relics were guarded by ravens. The same hospitality is still extended, and I am assured that the ravens still stand guard.

The evening services in the Mozarabe churches had a strong emotional appeal to Muslims brought up in the rigid and one

might almost say gymnastic ritual of their own faith.   The
lights, the incense and above all the administration of the
sacrament inspired several Andalusian poets.   How little they
understood the ceremony is clear from ibn Shuhayd's account
of what seems to have been a midnight mass in a church at
Cordoba.   It was carpeted with myrtle; the fire of devotion
warmed the church, and the tinkle of the bell rejoiced his ears.
"They take water not with cups but with the palms of their
hands from pillars. . . . How often in that church have I
breathed the scent of the young wine of youth, enhanced with
the bouquet of old age from the priest. . . . Young lads" (the
acolytes?) "toasted me with wine, blushing with modesty like
the tender gazelle under the eye of his lord. . . . They took
communion with him, these delicate lads, and he gave them
wine, and pork to eat."   The Mozarabe rite, like that of the
Church of England, comprehends communion in both kinds,
but there were clearly gaps in ibn Shuhayd's grasp of the ceremony he so thoroughly enjoyed.

These offices, stimulating as they were, were fraught with
peril for the good Muslim and particularly for his wife.   Ibn
Abdun, composing a manual of city government about the
same time, prescribed that Muslim women should not be
allowed into the churches, because the priests were rakes and
adulterers.   He went so far as to recommend that Frankish
women should be allowed to attend services only on formal
feast days, because they ate, drank and fornicated with the
priests, all of whom kept two or more at their disposal.   He
strongly favoured compulsory marriage for the priests, or at the
least circumcision.

The Feast of the Epiphany seems to have been kept in
Cordoba as in Egypt, the entire population joining in torch-
light processions that went on all night, and wearing fancy
dress.   It is not unlikely: the Andalusian loves to pass the
night in the streets;   one has only to spend Holy Week in
Seville or Malaga to see how untiring he is, particularly with
the extra excitement of dressing up.   It is not however recorded
whether convention required at Cordoba, as at Cairo, that
ladies of the town should wear trousers of scarlet leather.

Muslim feasts were observed with the same relish.   Besides
the standard days, they had the Persian Nawruz at the beginning of January, and Mihrajan, which they kept on Saint
John's Day instead of two months later.   They also made a
tremendous affair of marriages and circumcisions, including in
the latter festivities as many neighbours' boys as they could

find. No effort was spared to make it a memorable occasion; enormous sums were spent. There is no record of anything to touch Mutawakkil's expenditure of eighty-six million *dinars* at the circumcision of his son Mutazz by his favourite Qabiha; nevertheless in Spain the party given by Ma'mun ibn Dhu'l-Nun of Toledo for his grandson Yahya was so splendid that it remained a proverb as long as there were Muslims in Spain. Another Ma'mun, an Abbasid, gave a sumptuous feast on the occasion of his marriage with Bawran, the daughter of his Grand Vizir, the highlight being a rain of pearls that came up to the bride's chin.

Such feasts lasted a week or more and left no time for sleep. The same tireless appetite for enjoyment is a feature of the present-day *ferias* in Seville and Valencia; in fact Andalusians seem to be born with the faculty of doing without sleep.

These were great occasions; for everyday there was the stand-by of the garden party. Every family of any standing owned a *munya* or country seat: the whole plain between Cordoba and the Sierra Morena was carpeted with them. The first Abd al-Rahman set the fashion with a farm called al-Rusafa, in memory of his ancestral pleasance in Syria. The long summer days and nights were spent in the formal gardens that the poets were so fond of describing; they had no liking for natural scenery or "park-like grounds"; no Gothick ruins or romantic crags for them. The grandest mountains filled them with loathing; what they liked was amiable formal gardens in flat country, with channels of running water, paths carefully sanded or paved with bricks on edge in geometrical patterns, such as may be seen in the courtyard of the Cathedral at Seville or the Alcazbilla at Malaga and many other places; nature tamed by art to afford a cool fresh setting for social exchanges and *fêtes champêtres*. They were the same trim gardens dear in Elizabethan times to retired Leisure, neat rectangles with symmetrical flower-beds and avenues of trees like brussels sprouts that in happier days one used to see in the pictures hanging in muniment rooms.

Ibn Hazm describes an earthly paradise on the approved model: flower-beds overlooking a wide prospect, where the soul found refreshment: little streams crossing one another like swords of silver; birds singing full-throated: fruit for the plucking: shady branches screening the sun's rays: flowers of many colours stirred by the fragrant breeze: a spring day, the sun not too strong, veiled by a mist or light rain, like a shy maiden hiding herself from jealous eyes or discovering herself to her lover. It is the temperate paradise of dwellers in the sun-scorched desert.

Water devices were the *sine qua non* of garden planning. The same Ma'mun dhu'l-Nun is famous for an ingenious summer-house he had built in the middle of a lake: it was a domed edifice made of glass and gilt work; water was carried up to the top and allowed to fall in a transparent sheath, while Ma'mun sat cool and dry within. At night it was brilliantly lit up.

Their choice of flowers was limited: a list of those mentioned by the poets compiled by Pérès includes myrtle, daisies, violets, narcissus, blue iris, carnations, lilies, jonquils, waterlilies, red roses, jasmine and the red anemone: the blossoms of fruit-trees and broad beans also found admirers. They must have had many others that did not stir the poets' pulses: oranges were certainly known in the 11th century, for the bitter variety was supposed to carry a hoodoo for sovereigns. Badis at Granada kept a gardener solely to prevent any illwisher from planting one by stealth in his grounds.

Mu'tadid, king of Seville and father of the poet-king, laid out one terrace of his garden with a border of stakes, on which he fixed the skulls of his enemies. The credit for the design belongs to Mahdi, one of the ephemeral rulers of the *fitna*, who instructed his general, Wadih, to keep up a regular supply of what he used to say was kohl to his eyes. Mu'tadid introduced the refinement of a scroll inserted in the aural cavity and bearing a summary biography of the original owner. Besides this somewhat forbidding *parterre*, he kept a chestful indoors for private gloating, chiefly of Berbers. He wrote a poem on his hobby:

"The lances that gleamed in battle have become flowers in my garden;
 I have planted them as trees, and they bear splendid fruit."

His son did away with the outdoor collection, but was suspected of keeping the Berbers.

No modish garden could be without a gazebo. In his account of his youthful passion for a slave, ibn Hazm tells of a party at his parents' *finca*, where the women, after keeping out of sight during the heat of the day, climbed at sunset into a little tower, that commanded a view of Cordoba and the countryside, crowding to the windows and peeping through the shutters. The boy went to the window where she was, but she slipped away to another, and for all his pursuing he never came up with her. All with such graceful art that no-one saw, but she knew his love.

Sea travel in the
Middle Ages

A shop window

Aesthetic needs once satisfied, other appetites had to be catered for. The presentation of food, however, never received the earnest attention that has been lavished on it in Christian Europe; the whole dinner was put on the table at once, and the guests helped themselves to whatever they liked. There were some fresh ideas: rabbits were a staple diet, in spite of the Quranic prohibition, and no doubt other prescriptions of the Law were disregarded. The brown truffle was greatly prized by epicures and rakes (it was hopefully credited with aphrodisiac properties), but some of their choicest dishes are to our taste revolting: such horrors as stews spiced with musk and camphor. Certain refinements were initiated by the famous singer Ziryab, the *arbiter elegantiarum* of the court of Abd al-Rahman II; he invented snacks that could easily be detached and carried to the mouth, like force-meat balls and miniature *vol-au-vents*; he also introduced asparagus, and no doubt gave expensive demonstrations of its correct management at meals.

During the meal there was no conversation and no wine, but certain rules of procedure had to be observed. A well-bred guest would never think of extracting the marrow from a bone,[1] (though he could properly offer it to another guest), nor snatch the brain or kidneys or the chicken breast, if he was the first invited to fall to. It was also bad form to mix viands of different kinds, as is now the custom in the United States; but on the whole there was little ceremonial, certainly none of the holy modern ritual; eating was a necessary process, like stoking a furnace; the fun came later.

When the last guest was replete, and all had washed their hands in an adjoining room, the party settled down to the feast of reason and the flow of soul. The wine now made its appearance, accompanied by the *friandises* which were always served with it, nuts, olives, fruit, cheesecakes and such odd appetizers as edible earth, whatever it can have been, or sugar-cane soaked in rose-water. Conversation became general; at the best parties there would be not more than half-a-dozen guests, and those would spend the best part of the night "drinking of the limpid water of friendship and conviviality, offering each other the marrow of their hearts, spreading the carpet of mirth and loosening the bonds of formality". All this was made easy by the wine, served by a pretty slave-girl or a glamorous youth: countless love-poems were addressed to

---

[1] Omar Khayyam reserved this delicacy for the seclusion of a *tête-à-tête* in the country. In the famous quatrain that opens with "A book of verses .." Fitzgerald's "loaf of bread" is a marrow-bone in the original.

these Ganymedes, either sex being regarded as fair game by the Andalusians. In the most exquisite circles the cup-bearer might be a *ghulamiyya*, a neat young slave-girl dressed as a boy—an artifice designed to stimulate the more *blasé*.

The principal entertainment was provided by singing-girls and musicians. Their instruments may still be heard in Muslim countries—the lute, the *qanun* (grand-uncle of the zither), the rebec, a primitive violin, various flutes and wind instruments, and several kinds of drum. Purists regarded percussion instruments as vulgar; perhaps the prejudice survived from the Almohads' use of them in warfare. Ibn Hazm remarks that though it is nothing more than an empty skin, it engenders an intimidating noise, and I well remember the loathing I conceived for it one fiery summer in Marrakesh, when day or night one could never escape from it. A thousand years ago, an indignant father embalmed in comminatory couplets an errant son, who, not content with marrying a light woman, had even joined her orchestra.

"Not enough to fornicate and drink the heady new wine:
    Thou must even play the tambourine in public."

Music was taken very seriously: it was one of the subjects of the *quadrivium* at Cordoba, having been introduced by that versatile poet ibn Firnas in the 9th century. The course later covered al-Farabi's work on musical theory, itself based on two books by Euclid, on harmony and the graduation of the scale.

Monarchs themselves gave profound attention to music, theoretical and practical: the Caliph Hakam is credited with improvements to the *buq*, a long brass wind instrument with a reed. Musical therapeutics also came into the syllabus: the curative effect of music on the nerves has never lacked students since David gave his course of treatment to King Saul. The impact of music on the inflammable Arab temperament was always extreme; al-Ghazali went so far as to define "ecstasy" as the condition derived from listening to music: audiences were wont to gasp and froth at the mouth, to bite their thumbs and even to beat their heads on walls. Famous musicians rated their own achievements very high: it is related of a singer named Ma'bid, who performed at Walid's court in Damascus, that he took offence of the honours bestowed on a general, who had captured seven fortresses; saying that he had composed seven songs, any one of which was worth more than a wretched fortress.

There were however two schools of thought: the Prophet

himself did not approve of music, and from time to time the *faqihs* managed to get the prohibition enforced; but never very whole-heartedly, in spite of the terrifying *hadith* of the Miraj, describing Hell as seen by Muhammad through a tiny chink in the great door; there the musicians, lumped together igno- miniously with professional mourners, are hung up by their feet, braying like asses or barking like dogs, while devils slit their tongues with shears of fire.

Nevertheless music remained one of the principal distractions of Muslim Spain, as it was in Elizabethan England, in many particulars oddly like the Caliphate, where any barber's shop provided a set of instruments for the solace of waiting customers. Executants had a special chapter in the book of etiquette, and even a formal costume was prescribed for them, cut from a striped brocade called *washy* woven at Malaga: they wore their hair long, rouged their faces and hands heavily, and sometimes wore a cap with bells.

Their performances were listened to with critical and informed attention: the audience was all *cognoscenti*: even in his cups a cultivated Andalusian had a fine ear for poetry. The best singers could improvise verse to fit the occasion: ibn Qutiya tells the story of a big symposium given by Uthman, the son of the Amir Muhammad. His elder brother Ibrahim arrived in the middle, explaining that he had spent hours seek- ing for diversion and elegant conversation, but whatever door he knocked at, they told him the master was at Uthman's party, so he had invited himself to the entertainment. As he had already dined, Uthman turned to the curtain, which concealed the musicians, and called on Bacea, his best singer, to give them the cream of her *répertoire*. So she improvised and sang

> Only to see who visits thee, joy springs in my soul;
> My heart throbs with delight, looking on him who loves thee.

This was much more to Ibrahim's taste than Uthman's; and as soon as the party broke up, he gave the girl a sound thrashing. Some time later, when he was giving another party, Ibrahim again arrived, and Uthman again called on the girl, but this time she sang

> When I see the grimaces of this ugly bird, I can only bid him "Avaunt,
> Thou crow of ill omen, that comest between a lover and his beloved."

Ibrahim started up in fury, Uthman called for a whip and promised Bacea five hundred lashes: oil was poured on the commotion by an exquisite from Alexandria, who told Ibrahim

the whole story. He went off vowing never to enter his
jealous brother's house again, and whether the girl escaped her
thrashing is a matter for conjecture.

.   .   .   .   .

Malaga, then as now, was the home of song: the poet
Manuel Machado, calling the roll of the towns of Andalusia,
labels Malaga as "*cantaora*", which is "singer" in the local
dialect. Even to-day a charwoman washing the floor or
polishing the silver enlivens the work with oriental cadences:
the processions in Holy Week are punctuated by *saetas* supposed to be wrung from the bystanders by the beauty of the
scene, but perhaps the art is a little less unpremeditated than
that. In any case song is the vehicle in which the Malagueño
naturally expresses himself, morning, noon and night; and so
it was at the beginning of the 12th century when a distinguished
visitor fell ill at Malaga and had to keep his bed. "At night,"
he writes, "when darkness fell, my sleeplessness was aggravated
by the lutes and drums and lyres that sounded in all directions,
accompanied by the voices of singers, which irritated me and
added to my discomfort. I sought an apartment where I
would hear none of the voices and music, but without success;
such is the inveterate custom of the people of that region. But
one night being awakened from my first sleep, those hateful
and distracting noises for once were stilled, and a suave and
agreeable music stole on my ear, the like of which I had never
heard. The music became gradually louder, pursued by my
soul, until it reached its height; nevertheless I felt such solace
that I forgot my pain. Then I heard a voice, fresher than
flowers after rain." He rose from his sick-bed, went to the
window and saw an authentic *zambra* [1] (the Arabic word is still
current); there were a score of men, with fruit and drink before
them, and girls holding lutes, drums and flutes, but not playing;
and on one side the girl who was singing, her lute in her lap.
He listened enchanted and forgot his pains; the next day a
friend told him she was a *diva* from Bagdad, formerly a slave of
Mansur, who had passed to her present master with the collapse of the Empire.

.   .   .   .   .

In spite of the sternest prohibitions, the drinking of wine was
universal. It was quite ineffective to invent fearful penalties in
the next world; in the face of hair-raising visions of wine-

[1] Musical party.

bibbers howling for water and being served by devils with cups of liquid fire that melted the flesh from their faces, we have an unrepentant Muslim on his deathbed, who ought to have been imploring the pardon of the Most High, lifting his hands in supplication and saying with his last breath, "Oh Lord of all things in Paradise, I only ask thee for a draught of Malaga wine." There is an impressive body of Anacreontic verse, which seems more sincere than most Arabic poetry. One of the last Umayyad princes sang,

"I have passed my life among drinkers and lovely faces; I have not wasted
     one evening or dawn:
  My nights I spend awake in drunken revels, and I never hear the morning
     muezzin call me to fresh pleasures."

At the close of the 11th century the Andalusians came in for severe castigation on account of their intemperance at the hands of two famous warriors. The first was the Cid, in his address to the Valencians after the capture of their city, promised to do justice on two days of the week, regularly; "but if your case be urgent, come to me any day, and I will hear you; for I do not spend my time with women, drinking and singing, like your masters, whom you cannot see when you need them." At much the same time the Almoravid Yusuf al-Tashufin, who was hammering at the other gate, obtained from the doctors of religion a *fetwa* condemning the princes as debauched and impious and meriting deposition. There is no room for doubt that this censure was well earned, for even judges, who were chosen for their moral qualities, were guilty of occasional, and maybe regular lapses. There is a spirited account of quite inappropriate behaviour on the part of two leading qadis at one of their bi-weekly meetings at the house of the vizir Muhalabi. When the party warmed up, each took a cup of wine from Qatrabbul, dipped his white beard in it and aspersed the other guests, perhaps a reminiscence of those Christian rites that so much interested them.

The trouble was that the Prophet had omitted to legislate for the sin of drunkenness. The Quran contains a corpus of law covering most common offences, but the Hijaz not being a wine-growing country, drunkenness was infrequent, and no precise penalty had been laid down. The leading case was inconclusive: a man who had drunk wine being brought before the Prophet, he directed that he should be given a beating, and the offender got off with a few slaps with a slipper. Later on, when Ali was consulted, he took a far severer view. "Whoso drinks," he said, "gets drunk: whoso gets drunk acts foolishly: whoso acts foolishly lies: whoso lies deserves the punishment": assessing the punishment at eighty lashes. This might have been a powerful deterrent (if ever a man took thought before getting drunk), but many judges balked at the stern sentence, and did their best to look the other way. The Book of the Judges of Cordoba contains many such stories. One qadi on his mule, finding himself behind an intoxicated man weaving along a narrow street, checks his mount to a snail's pace until the man reels into a side passage; another while committing a man to prison nudges a bystander and whispers, "Ask me to let him off." A third confronted with a delinquent asks the watch, "Does he smell of wine?" and when they say he does, turns to a looker-on and asks, "Is it sure?" He answers, "He smells of something," and the judge dismisses him for want of corroboration.

The Christian taverns were such a temptation. They were often next to the church, and kept by women, usually accommodating in other respects. "How many wine-wives have I awakened," sings the poet, "when the pearl necklace of the morning dew was broken." The morning cup was accounted the best, on the principle of a hair of the dog: so to-day a good Spaniard breakfasts on a swig of red wine, with or without a roll fried in olive oil.

The *faqihs* however fought a grim battle and scored an occasional victory. In the 11th century ibn Jahwar is praised by a court poet for breaking all the wine-jars in Cordoba, a feat beyond any official's power. Once they succeeded in persuading the sovereign to uproot all the vineyards in Andalusia, but he desisted when wiser men warned him that if he did so, more violent poisons would be brewed. There is mention of another product of the vine, called "nabid",[1] which may have been a variety of that spirit, which is drunk all over the Levant under the names of araq, raki, ouzo, suma, chipuro and the rest. One sort is still drunk in Andalusia, with an added flavouring of aniseed. It may however have been nothing more pernicious than grape-juice, for at the famous feast of Ma'mun it was offered as a soft drink.

Parties usually lasted till dawn; if they broke up earlier, there was danger from the Watch, which came on duty after the night prayer. There was a picturesque survival of this watch in Marrakesh not so long ago: the *mukhaznis* met at midnight in the great square of the Jum' al-Fna, and proceeded

[1] "Nbid" is the vernacular word for wine in Syria.

to patrol the city, first firing a volley from their muskets to apprise malefactors of their setting out. In Cordoba it was the duty of the watch to arrest anyone found loitering in the streets at night, and to put him in the lock-up till morning. It was however laid down that if their capture was a person of distinction, they should either escort him to his house, or put him into a decent *fonda* for what remained of the night.

An occasional attraction at parties was conjuring. Dance-girls used to juggle with sabres and daggers, but there are also mentions of a professional "*khayali*" or illusionist, often of Egyptian origin. From what little is written about them, they were not on the level of that accomplished Galli-Galli, who used to come on board at Port Said and extract day-old chickens from his eyebrows. The only tricks specifically described concern vanishing bottles and glasses, and that leaves a lurking suspicion.[1]

Another game was "*kurraj*", "little horses"; the frequent enthusiastic references to it arouse but do not appease one's curiosity. It was played with some kind of little horse, fastened in some way to the skirts of dancing-girls. How it was played is not known, but it certainly excited the greatest con-centration. One of Mu'tamid's captains was so enthralled by a game that he was caught by an enemy detachment; pre-sumably his sentries were also deep in the game. I have wondered whether it at all resembled a carnival dance I used to see in Athens, in which the performer had a horse built round his middle, its feet just clear of the ground, and gave an effective exhibition of *haute école*.

Chess, backgammon and draughts were all common recrea-tions, and did not escape the censure of the godly. Ibn Abdun recommends that they should be banned, as games of chance and a sin, which keep the good Muslim from his religious duties. He couples them with another game called "arrows", but I fear it would be presumptuous to regard it as a precursor of to-day's darts.

[1] Lévi-Provençal says the *khayali* dealt in "*ombres chinoises*", for which I know no English equivalent. He throws shadows on a screen, to the accompaniment of dialogue. In Turkey and Greece he is known as *Karaghiöz*.

CHAPTER TEN

PORTRAIT GALLERY

ABD AL-RAHMAN AL-DAKHIL, THE FOUNDER
(8th century)

THE LABYRINTHINE course of Arab history is made a little less perplexing by attentively following the clue of kinship. The ties of family always played a dominant rôle in the intricate shifts of policy, the alliances and rebellions, the rise and decline of dynasties. They are the mainspring of every form of activity: disloyalty to one's kin is the unpardonable sin. "Accursed is he that boasts of kinship to a family that is a stranger to him," said the Prophet, "accursed he that denies his benefactor." The tie is perpetual and extends beyond those born in the tribe to all clients and freedmen who have been adopted into it.[1]

Spain had been conquered while the Umayyad Caliphs reigned in Damascus, and many of their kindred had followed the victorious armies; many Spaniards had been converted to Islam under their patronage and so incurred a debt of tribal gratitude. "Love thy tribe," says the Law, "for thou art joined to thy tribe by closer bonds than a man to his wife." This was the reasoning that brought Abd al-Rahman to Spain, where he founded the Western Caliphate.

The Umayyads had reigned in Damascus for a century, drawing their strength from Syria and in return giving Syria a period of splendour and prosperity that was never to be repeated. When Hisham died in 743, they committed suicide by forgetting the paramount importance of loyalty to family and tribe: in seven years four Caliphs defended the uneasy throne against pretenders of their own blood: the last of them signed

---

[1] The Arabs took their feuds with them wherever they went; the principal divisions referred back to battles where the tribes had taken different sides. The battle at Siffin between Ali and Mu'awiya, that of Harra between Mecca-Medina and Damascus, and that of Merj-Rahit between Qaisi and Yemeni set up many planes of cleavage that were only healed when the tribes had lost all corporate sense. The tribes most often mentioned in these pages are the Yemenis and Kelbis, usually on the Umayyad side, and the Ma'adi, Madari and Qaisi on the other. The former group traced their ancestry back to Qahtan the son of Shem, the latter to Adman the son of Ismail, thus giving the feud a venerable though improbable antiquity.

the death warrant of the dynasty, when he turned his back on
Syria and sought support in Iraq. In 750 the Abbasids found the
conditions favourable for the revolution they had been plotting
for years, striking down not only the Umayyads but also the
family of Ali, whose claim to the legitimate succession they had
espoused as long as it suited them; and setting up in Bagdad
their own dynasty, which was to last for some five centuries.

The new Caliph, Abu Abbas, was represented in Syria by
an uncle, who called himself al-Saffah—the shedder of blood,
the generous host whose pride it is to slaughter cattle to enter-
tain his guests: he now proceeded to justify his sobriquet in a
new and grimmer sense. Wherever his officers could search
out members of the Umayyad family, they were subjected to
every ignominy or slaughtered out of hand. "Having captured Aban ibn Mu'awiya," says the *Akhbar Majmu'a*, the
collected traditions, "they cut off a foot and a hand and sent
him round the regions of Syria" (where he had been loved and
respected as a great nobleman) "and a cryer with him crying,
'This is Aban ibn Mu'awiya, the best horseman of the Banu
Umayya', until he died. They killed the women and children,
against all the customs, and beheaded Abda the daughter of
Hisham, because when they asked of her jewels and treasures,
she answered not a word."

The family went into hiding, until al-Saffah proclaimed an
amnesty. "They wrote that the Commander of the Faithful
was heavy-hearted because of what had come to pass with the
Banu Umayya, and wished to leave them their lives, and had
given orders to provide them with safe-conducts, that none
should molest them or stand in their way." Some seventy of
the survivors swallowed the bait, and were murdered in circumstances that have not ceased to horrify the chroniclers. "As
they arrived, al-Saffah gathered them in his tent, and when all
were there, he took Abd al-Wahid"—the senior member
present—"and made him sit next to him, as if to show the
gratitude which the Abbasids owed them, and talked to him of
that matter and made great cheer. Then he made a sign to
the guards that stood behind them and said, 'Beat their heads
in,' and at once they were killed with clubs. Then he said to
Abd al-Wahid, 'There is no reason why thou shouldst outlive
thy kinsfolk and their power, but I will grant thee the boon to
die by the sword'; and they beheaded him. And others say
that he had leather cloths [1] spread over the bodies of the dead
men, and feasted thereon."

[1] The usual covering for the dinner-table.

Abd al-Rahman ibn Mu'awiya, grandson of the Caliph Hisham, was wise enough not to attend this function, but stayed at his farm near the Euphrates. We have his own account of his escape, stored up in the adhesive memory of some Arab, who passed it on to the chronicler, and so preserved it for twelve centuries. He was meditating flight to North Africa and Spain: "By God, I wanted nothing but the West," on account of an incident that he remembered from when his father died. They took him with his brothers to al-Rusafa to see his grandfather. The great Maslama ibn Abd al-Malik was there, and when he heard they were the orphans of Mu'awiya, he called them in turn, and when he came to Abd al-Rahman, he took him on his saddle, and began to kiss him and to weep bitterly. Hisham came out and Maslama said to him, "The fulfilment is at hand: this is he: I have seen the signs in his face and neck." As so often happens, the narrator vouchsafes no explanation: clearly there was a prophecy of the fall of the dynasty and its re-establishment in the West.

Abd al-Rahman had had no warning of the arrival of the Abbasi troops; he was sitting in the shade bathing his eyes on account of some irritation, and his little son who was playing at the door ran to him and hid his face in his robes; he saw the Abbasi banner, and at the same moment his young brother ran to warn him. They snatched up some money and galloped to the Euphrates, followed by the soldiers, and plunged in. The Abbasis called them back, saying they had nothing to fear. "I continued to swim, and my brother a little behind me. I turned to help him and encourage him to join me, but alas! on hearing those words of peace he had turned back for fear of drowning, hastening to his death. I called to him, 'Come here, beloved', but God did not will that he should hear me, and he went back. Some of the enemy began to strip and swim after me, but they gave up, and took the boy and cut his head off before me. He was thirteen years old: may God have had pity on him! I went on."

He made his way to Palestine, where a freedman named Badr found him and brought him money and jewels from his sisters, eventually reaching the Maghrib, where he had many kin. Here another prophecy came near to undoing him. The governor was one Abd al-Rahman ibn Abd al-Aziz; a Jewish astrologer had told him that one day Spain would be ruled by an Abd al-Rahman of royal blood, with two curls on his forehead. The governor proceeded to grow the curls, until the Jew reminded him that he was not of the blood royal; but when the real Abd al-Rahman was presented, he saw his curls and said, "By God, this is the man, but I will kill him." In fact he did kill some of Abd al-Rahman's relatives and seized their property, but Abd al-Rahman himself escaped to the Berber country, and after many tribulations reached the coast, where he found a temporary refuge with his mother's tribe.

From here he wrote to his kinsmen in Spain; they consulted the friendly chiefs and also a Qaisi leader named al-Sumayl, who was under obligations to the Umayyads and had a score to pay off on the Abbasi governor. The chronicler gives us a thumb-nail portrait of this swashbuckler, an illiterate drunkard and arrogant beyond belief, but brilliant and untiring and utterly without scruples. It was largely by his support that the governor, Yusuf al-Fikri, had become the master of Andalus; and Yusuf had characteristically rewarded him by sending him to Zaragoza to bring the Yemeni tribes to heel. Al-Sumayl found himself besieged and in great danger from the Yemenis (as Yusuf had hoped) and had to look for help. The Umayyads, with whom Badr was at that time negotiating, responded to the call and raised the siege. Sumayl rewarded them fittingly: two hundred *dinars* to each chief, fifty to each noble, ten to every soldier, with a bolt of cloth to all; so that they were in funds. The moment was auspicious for presenting Abd al-Rahman's letter to al-Sumayl, whose influence would have been decisive. At first he was ready to help him, but changed his mind on reflection, and eventually threw in his lot with Yusuf al-Fikri.

However the general response was just encouraging enough for the Umayyad party to send a boat to fetch Abd al-Rahman; the first man off was one Tammam ibn Alqama al-Ghalib, a fortunate omen—Abd al-Rahman punned happily on the first and last names, the radicals of which mean completion and conquest: "Our plan will be perfected and we will conquer our enemies." The Berbers however opposed the departure, and had to be bought off, "each receiving a gift without exception according to his standing". Even so, when the ship was casting off, yet another Berber arrived and laid hold of the cable; but one of the party, sick of the haggling, drew a sword and cut his hand off. There were no more adventures till Abd al-Rahman landed at Almuñecar in 755 after five years of wandering.

Meanwhile Yusuf and al-Sumayl, after defeating the Yemenis at Zaragoza "and cutting off all dangerous heads", were returning to Cordoba in high feather, when their confidence was shaken by news of Abd al-Rahman's landing. They decided to fall on him at once, but the troops had had enough of campaigning and deserted in a body. Al-Sumayl still pressed for immediate attack, but "the winter drew near, it came on to rain and the rivers rose and they turned to Cordoba, following the advice of those that spoke for a parley".

An embassy was accordingly despatched, with gifts, and would have succeeded but for the fatuous conduct of one of the mission; both parties spent the winter calling out their supporters. In the spring Abd al-Rahman marched round the country, but did not meet with any outstanding success, for the chiefs hung back. Only the Yemenis were with him, smarting from their reverse at Zaragoza, and eager for revenge. When they reached Seville and had news that Yusuf had marched from Cordoba against them, the time had come to swear allegiance to his banner: he improvised one from a turban fastened to a lance belonging to a man from the Hadramaut, "whose name is not known but they accounted it auspicious", and all took the oath in the farm of Calomera in the district of Tocina.

There was a ford at Tocina, and the two armies stood on either side, the water being too high to cross. Abd al-Rahman stole away at midnight, thinking to reach Cordoba and raise his supporters, but Yusuf got wind of it and moved after him, so that at sunrise the two armies still faced one another across the river, "like challenging stallions". They continued to march along the banks as far as Almazara, where there was a passable ford, Abd al-Rahman's troops tired and hungry, but Yusuf's well found. However when it was put to the vote, to treat or to fight, they voted for battle, and Abd al-Rahman crossed the river unopposed, under pretext of coming to terms; Yusuf sent cattle and sheep, and the two armies messed together, nobody doubting that peace would be made on the morrow. But the next day, the anniversary of the battle of Merj Rahit, which gave the Umayyads the Caliphate, Abd al-Rahman changed his front, and the armies met in battle.

In the middle of it the Yemenis seeing him mounted on a mettlesome horse said, "This is a young stripling: who is our surety that he will not gallop away and leave us to die?" He thereupon called one Abu Sabbah, who had an ancient mule that had been dapple-grey but was now white, and said to him, "There is no mule in the host more to my liking than thine: this horse is very restive, and I cannot discharge my arrows as I

wish. Take him and I will take thy mule, for I would ride a
steed that all can see, lest they turn their backs in flight."
This little bit of histrionics put fresh heart into the Yemenis;
they charged again and routed the enemy right and centre;
Yusuf and Sumayl ran; the left with the Qaisis stood till
evening, when all the chiefs were dead.

After sacking Yusuf's camp and banqueting on his provisions,
Abd al-Rahman marched to Cordoba without encountering
more opposition; he found Yemenis looting Yusuf's house, and
gave protection to the defeated enemy's household. Yusuf
himself continued the struggle, until his partisans abandoned
him in defeat; his following was reduced at last to a single
slave, with whom he was riding to Toledo, when one Abdallah
al-Ansari recognized him and killed him, so that the people
might rest from his evil-doing.

Abd al-Rahman was now Amir in Cordoba, but for thirty
years he had to defend his title against Abbasid attempts to
reimpose their authority, and an endless series of revolts from
the turbulent population. In 763 an Abbasid governor named
Mughit, aided by the Yemenis, now indisposed towards him,
shut him up in Carmona for two months, but he made a desperate sortie and broke the besieging armies, afterwards sending
the Abbasid Caliph the heads of Mughit and his chief officers.
A few years later he had to deal with a serious revolt of the
Berbers, which meant seven years campaigning; in 777 he faced
a coalition in the north which brought in Charlemagne himself. The principal rebel got as far as Murcia before Abd
al-Rahman had him murdered; Charlemagne, having crossed
the Pyrenees, was forced by domestic troubles to return, when
his rear-guard was cut to pieces at Roncesvalles by the wild
ancestors of the Basques, enriching literature with the *Chanson
de Roland*.

As he strengthened his hold on the country, more waverers
flocked to his standard, but he came to depend largely on a
standing army of Berber mercenaries, whom he brought over
from the Maghrib. For the rest a strong hand, lightning decision, ruthless chastisement or politic clemency, and assassina-
tion when there was nothing else for it, enabled him at last to
leave his son Hisham a country well in hand, which contained
the seeds of power and prosperity.

Here is a composite portrait of him from several sources. He
was tall and fair, with hollow cheeks: he had lost an eye and
had a mole on his face. He wore his hair in two plaits, and had
a moustache, which it was his habit to tug when his patience

was wearing thin.   He was never idle, and rarely long at rest:
he relied on his own intelligence and did not leave the conduct
of affairs to others.   He was capable of reckless courage, as of
extreme prudence;   like most of his family he was extremely
accessible, and used to mix freely with the people, until his
friends pointed out the evil of too great familiarity.   He was
sharply criticized for his ingratitude to the freedman Badr, who
had done him such great service in his early struggles: ibn
Hayyan says that he treated those that rebelled against him
better than those that helped him.   He dressed always in
white, had eleven sons and nine daughters, spoke with facility
and elegance and was a poet on his day.

His life was summed up in an anecdote of the Abbasid
Caliph Mansur, his contemporary and enemy.   One day he
asked his friends, "Who is the Falcon of the Quraish?" [1]   They
replied that it was himself, the Commander of the Faithful,
because he organized the Empire, put down revolt and gave
peace to men's minds.   Then they suggested Mu'awiya and
Abd al-Malik, both great sovereigns, but he said, "It is Abd
al-Rahman ibn Mu'awiya, who first by cunning escaped from
among the spears and swords of his enemies, traversed the desert
and crossed the sea, entered a land of Unbelievers, founded
cities, gathered armies and with his good government and
firmness of character built an empire in a lawless country.
Mu'awiya rode a steed which Umar and Uthman had made
ready for him: Abd al-Malik had been proclaimed before he
succeeded: the Commander of the Faithful had the support of
his family and partisans: but Abd al-Rahman was alone, with
nothing to aid him but his wits, and no supporter but his
unshakable will."

UMAR IBN HAFSUN, THE REBEL
(9th century)

The last lap of the railway journey from Madrid to Malaga
is exciting.   Since first thing in the morning trains from the
four quarters have been hobnobbing at Bobadilla, the junction
in the middle of a featureless plain, while their passengers
played at General Post: at last the Malaga train tears itself
away, and moves off southwards towards a row of unimpressive
hills: the driver, bent on making up time, takes advantage of
the gradient to put on speed, and dives into a longish tunnel,
from which the train debouches into a stretch of fantastic

[1] The Prophet's tribe, from which the ruling lines all claimed descent.

landscape, the gorge of the Chorro. There are fourteen more tunnels, mostly short; between them the passenger gets glimpses of perpendicular cliffs with sudden deep valleys. On the right a narrow catwalk, a yard wide, plastered on the sheer rock, runs level with the train, finally crossing a rift like a sword-cut six hundred feet deep as the train slows down in the Chorro station. This is where the hydro-electric works now provide Malaga with power: high above on the forbidding *meseta* of Villaverde stand the ruins of Bobastro, where Umar ibn Hafsun built his eyrie a thousand-odd years ago.

Nowadays the climb is not too strenuous: the Department of Afforestation has been planting trees and carrying out flood-protection works, and one of their tracks makes a pleasant approach to the site, giving the pilgrim time to study the scenic chaos of naked rocks and appraise the immense natural strength of the position. Once at the summit, he dominates the whole countryside and has a clear view along the valley of the Guadalhorce, which was the only possible approach of any considerable force.

Of the impregnable fortress that crowned Bobastro, little can be identified beyond confused foundations; but lower down, where a narrow ledge hangs on the edge of the void, there stands the skeleton of his church, hewn out of the living rock. The ground-plan is a basilica, about fifty feet by thirty-five, with three aisles, an apse, and squarish chapels on either side of it: the site selected is a hummock shaped like the top of a Dutch cheese: starting from north and west, the limestone has been extracted, leaving the exterior walls and the piers and arches of the nave standing free; the work was never completed, the south and west walls are still embedded in the rock. This is the enigmatic monument left by the great *caudillo* who led revolt against the Umayyads, and came near to overthrowing the Amirate five hundred years before its time.

Umar was born at Iznate near Ronda in 860, of a noble Vizigoth family, which had embraced Islam two generations before. Ibn Hayyan gives his pedigree: Umar ibn Hafsun ibn Ja'far (who apostatized) ibn Shetim (Septimus?) ibn Fergalush (Fregellus) ibn Comes (Count) Adefonso. Umar's youth was wild: he seems to have led a sort of gang warfare against his Arab neighbours, in the course of which he either killed one and had to run, or was caught and flogged by an Arab official, and then kicked out of the house by his father. He went into hiding at Tahurt in the Maghrib, taking up the improbable trade of assistant to a tailor who came from his village. One day an old man came into the shop with a length of cloth, and settling down to the customary chat asked who Umar was, and hearing that he came from Rayya [1] asked him if he knew Bobastro. Umar confessing that he used to live in the hills below, the old man went on, "Is there any rebellion?" "No," replied Umar. "There soon will be," said the old man. "Know you a man named Umar ibn Hafsun?" Then looking straight at Umar, whom he had known at once by a missing tooth, lost in one of his affrays, "Wretch!" he said, "you try to fill your belly working with a needle: go back to your country: you shall be the master of the Umayyads and drive them to destruction, and be the king of a great kingdom." "Thereupon Umar, fearing that the lords of Tahurt, who were clients of the Banu Umayya, might lay hold of him, put two loaves in his sleeve and so came to Spain." Afraid to face his father, he went to his uncle Mudhahir, who helped him to gather some forty like-minded young bloods, and soon made himself master of the Bobastro country.

The time was propitious: on all sides the country-born whether Christian or renegade, were sick of the arrogance of the Arabs; the Amir Muhammad was a weakling, of whom even the court historians could find nothing more flattering to record than that he was a notable arithmetician and could unerringly track down the smallest mistake in the accounts Toledo, the ancient capital of the Vizigoths, kept up a running fight that ended in the Amir granting the town something like republican status: in the Upper Marches the *muwallad* family of the Banu Qasi were all but independent: in the west Merwan the Galician, another *muwallad*, was master of Badajoz and treated with Muhammad on terms of easy contempt. Though none of these was conscious of leading a national crusade it was no less; but although from time to time they joined forces for an immediate purpose, the idea of concerted action for the establishment of native Spanish rule was out of their range. The Amir was thus able to maintain some figment of authority by dealing with them piecemeal: a treaty here, a campaign there, brought one or other to heel, while Hashim the Amir's favourite and wazir, concentrated his forces against the most pressing danger.

Even in victory he seldom dared do more than pardon the rebel and swear him to fealty; and so it happened that after a couple of years Umar capitulated and led his band to Cordoba

[1] The area round Ronda: Latin Regia.

The Fountain of the Lions in the Alhambra

Ivory caskets of
the Caliphate

where they enlisted in the Amir's army, and soon distinguished themselves in a battle at Poncorvo against the Banu Qasi, so winning Hashim's favour. This unfortunately brought with it the hostility of the *zalmedina*, Walid ibn Ganem, rival and enemy of Hashim, who lost no opportunity of doing Umar a disservice, allotting him the least attractive quarters, and issuing to his troop nothing but the poorest rations. This treatment Umar found intolerable; one day he took some uneatable corn to Walid: "*Hombre*, God be merciful to you, can a man live eating such filth?" but meeting with an insolent rebuff, he gathered his forty partisans and rode to Bobastro, seized the fortress which Hashim had built, ejected the commander and took his daughter (or mistress perhaps) to wife.

So began thirty years of revolt: his soldiers were all native Spaniards, some of whom had kept their Christian faith and others apostatized. The record is confused, the chroniclers putting the outstanding events in different sequence: but when he was at his zenith, his writ ran through all Andalusia south of the Guadalquivir: in Granada, Archidona, Osuna, Baena, Ecija and Aguilar his word was law: ibn Hajjaj of Seville and ibn Mastana of Jaen were his allies: his scouts raided up to the walls of Cordoba and threw their javelins at the statue that still stood over the Gate of the Bridge. "And all this," the chronicler confesses, "without much following or wealth or equipment, but he served as a scourge in the hands of God, who used him to make manifest his judgment on his people. . . He appeared in a time of commotion, when hearts were hardened and inclined to wickedness, and malignant spirits sought occasion of evildoing and civil warfare; and he found the people like-minded with him and disposed to make common cause with him."

The people indeed, who in those inhospitable mountains had suffered little admixture of Arab blood, rallied at once to his standard when he proclaimed that he sought for nothing but to give them justice, and relieve them of the crushing burdens the Arabs had laid on them; with the people thus heart and soul with him, his rule was kindly, firm and just. "Within his dominion a woman could travel alone with all her possessions, and none dared molest her." This was achieved by impartial severity: the punishment of theft was usually death, and his own son was as liable to punishment as any other. The odds indeed were loaded in favour of the victim, for his evidence was accepted without question. Towards his soldiers he was a father: to his best fighters he awarded a golden bracelet; he

L

had a warm spot in his heart for a valiant enemy, and made friend of him as soon as he had defeated him.

The detailed history of his revolt is of limited interest even t specialists: it is a dog-fight over all Andalus: castles and town are besieged, captured and recaptured: Umar forays as fa as Jaen, captures the governor of Priego: his bands ravagin the Iznajar country are defeated by the Amir's general, and pu to the sword. Ibn Idhari recounts the swaying fortune of th long-drawn-out struggle. Mundhir (who succeeds Muham mad and has worse luck than he deserves) captures two castle of the region of Malaga with those of Cabra, and marches on t besiege Bobastro "from very near", after devastating the sur rounding country: goes off to Archidona, which is held b Umar's friend Ayshun, reducing the garrison to such straits tha they hand over Ayshun's partisans, who are sent to Cordob to be crucified next to the Bab al-Sudda: Ayshun himsel between a dog and a pig, "because he was wont to boast tha if the Amir could catch him, he was welcome to crucify hin with a pig on his right and a dog on his left". Mundhi obliged him in this particular, though no-one could approve o the way he caught him, for "being unable to take him in fai fight, he bought the complicity of a man of Archidona, wh captured him by breaking the law of hospitality".

Umar had his little jokes too. When Mundhir pressed hin hard in Alhama, he asked for a parley and promised to be th Amir's loyal subject; Mundhir signed an amnesty and gav the sons of Umar, who had negotiated the treaty, very preciou clothes, loading the pack-animals with gold and other present for them. Umar then asked for a hundred mules, to brin his household and their effects to Cordoba; the Amir sent then with an honourable escort of ten officers and a hundred an fifty horse. All these Umar sent to Bobastro, where his famil was, and the doctors who had drawn up the treaty had the camp broken up, convinced that this was the end of the trouble, bu Umar galloped from Alhama to throw himself into Bobastro ejected the officers and seized the mules and returned to hi old ways.

Then Mundhir swore never to give up the siege until he hac Umar in fetters, but fell ill and sent for his brother Abdallah tc take over the conduct of the siege; he died soon after his brothe arrived, some say of poison which the latter brought with him At the sovereign's death the army melted away, and Abdallal had difficulty in keeping even a decent escort, and had to asl Umar not to molest what was now only a funeral procession

Umar gallantly contented himself with sacking the Amir's camp.

So it went on: presently Umar offered to do homage to Abdallah, on condition of remaining in Bobastro with a sort of Resident to represent the Amir's authority. This lasted as long as it suited Umar, but eventually the Resident was stripped and expelled. Then comes a surprising *coup de théâtre*: Abdallah is shut up in Cordoba, with Servando at Poley, waiting for the fall of the capital: Umar seems to be invincible, and treats with ibn Aghlab, the Abbasid governor of the Maghrib, to be accepted as the Amir of Andalus. Abdallah, no fighter but desperate, decides to lead a forlorn hope against the rebel, and pitches his tent outside the gates, as is the custom, for the troops to assemble. Umar, who had that day won one victory, is set on risking a *coup de main* and seizing the royal tent, and so inflicting a humiliation from which Abdallah could never recover. But the battle goes inexplicably against Umar, and he is forced to retreat to Cabra.

This is the turn of the tide: from that date (898) the chroniclers are more cheerful; "the rebel gravely wounded had to withdraw and retrace his steps in steep places, to endure shame and humiliation, and return broken and abased to Bobastro". Perhaps a little more cheerful than events warranted, for after the disaster Umar raised a new army and captured Elvira, the chief town in the plain of Granada. The Amir, says the chronicler, sent ibn Abi Abda after him, who destroyed him entirely: none the less he goes on to record between 900 and 914 nine more campaigns ending in complete victory against the beaten rebel; but he died in his bed in 918, unrepentant.

His star however had declined since the great defeat at Poley, and he hastened its eclipse by a very impolitic move in 899, when he publicly professed Christianity, and was baptized in the name of Samuel. His motives are obscure: he gained nothing by doing so; in the eyes of his *muwallad* supporters it was unforgivable, and it brought him no new accession of strength from the Christians. Either he acted on sincere conviction, or perhaps it was the surrender of a tired man to the importunity of his wife and daughter, both of them saints in the catholic calendar. According to Padre Flores [1] when his wife Columba died, his daughter Argentea, who had received solid instruction in the faith, pestered her father to make her a hermitage in the alcazar; he long refused, needing her services in the

---

[1] España Sagrada, vol. X, 466 and 564.

more worldly business of housekeeping, but finally gave way
and probably began then to hew the church out of the rock
He died before the work was finished, perhaps abandoned
before he died; something went wrong, for the piers on the
north side of the nave are out of alignment. Perhaps partie
working from opposite ends failed to make a perfect junction
if so, a symptom of his waning power.[1]

Ibn Idhari writes his epitaph with gusto. "In this year die
Umar ibn Hafsun, prop of the infidels, chief of hypocrites, fire
brand of civil war, refuge of the breeders of discord and hatred
This event was held a motive of rejoicing, a portent of divin
concern and the end of the reign of abomination."

It was nevertheless not quite the end of revolt: it took all th
skill and pertinacity of al-Nasir himself to make an end of th
sons of Umar, Hafs and Sulayman. Seven campaigns in seve
years and the systematic destruction of crops brought Hafs t
despatch the usual offer of submission. The Caliph ignored i
and "pursued with ardour and resolution his plan of siege
felled what remained of fruit-trees and vines and denied hi
enemies all means of life. He spent seven days from dawn til
night destroying everything and laying waste the countrysid
without mercy, and did likewise with the rebels' other castles.
This brought Hafs out to kneel at his feet: he gave him an
amnesty, as was his wont.

Then he went off to reduce the difficult country round
Almuñecar, but had to return to help Sulayman, whom he had
left in Bobastro: there had been another rising of the garrison
and Sulayman had been thrown out. He got in again, dis
guised as a woman, and turned the tables on the mutineers
"in this way Allah moved the infidels to destroy one another
so that no trace should remain".

Umar's sons rebelled once more in 926: Sulayman was killed
and his body gibbeted at the gate of al-Sudda. "That yea
there was a great drought and famine. . . . Rain fell when the
body of Sulayman was hung up, and the poets all wrote poem
contrasting the pure and beneficent rain from heaven with the
foul blood that dripped from the infidel carcass".

One more campaign in 927 brought Hafs at last to heel; the
Sultan again pardoned him and buried the past. He went to
Bobastro to survey the works that had for so long defied him

---

[1] Argentea went to Cordoba with her brother Hafs, when he finally
submitted in 928; three years later, according to Simonet, she died for he
faith, achieving the double crown of virgin and martyr, and was buried in
the Cathedral of the Three Saints.

nd returned thanks for the victory, fasting as long as he was
here. He set about building a new citadel of unparalleled
strength, and in deference to the *faqihs* had the bodies of Umar
nd his father exhumed; they were found to be lying on their
backs according to the Christian practice, so they were carried
back to the Bab al-Sudda and exposed with Sulayman's body,
" to serve as a salutary warning to some", crows ibn Idhari,
" and a pleasant spectacle to believers". And there they hung
or fifteen years until a great flood carried them away.

ZIRYAB, THE MUSICIAN
(9th century)

What brought him to Cordoba in the first place is not quite
certain: ambition, without doubt; but ambition might not by
tself have driven him to face the discomforts of the long journey
o Spain, if there had not been an additional spur; and that
was probably the belief that to remain in the familiar splendours
of Bagdad involved greater hazards than an excursion into the
unknown.

Dozy, the founder of the study of Muslim Spain, tells the
story in this way. Ziryab was the pupil of the celebrated
Ishaq al-Mausili at Bagdad. The Caliph Harun al-Rashid
inquiring whether Ishaq had no new singer, he replied, "I have
a disciple who sings well, thanks to my teaching, and I trust
will one day do me credit." The Caliph ordered him to be
sent to the palace, where he made the best impression. He
knew his own value: "I can sing all that others can sing," he
said, "also what they cannot. My art is only appropriate to
an accomplished *virtuoso* like the Presence." He refused his
master's lute, insisting on his own as the only instrument in
harmony with his superlative talent. Harun al-Rashid,
enchanted by his performance, rewarded him lavishly and
rated Ishaq for keeping the genius to himself. Ishaq excused
himself on the plea that it was Ziryab who had not revealed his
talent until the Presence had inspired him, and lost no time in
arriving at an understanding with his too brilliant pupil,
giving him the immediate choice between establishment elsewhere at his master's expense, or competition with him at
Bagdad with all its attendant risks. Ziryab was wise enough to
choose the former, and when the Caliph again called for him,
Ishaq explained that Ziryab, who regarded himself as a transcendent genius, had taken umbrage at the Caliph's inadequate

appreciation of his powers and left the country in a huff
consoling the Presence with the reflection that the genius wa
liable to fits of madness, during which he was dreadful to se
and capable of any enormity.

A different story is told by ibn Qutiyah; [1] Ziryab had been a
intimate of the Caliph Amin, the son of Harun al-Rashid, bu
Ma'mun, who succeeded Amin, "reproached him certai
matters" and he fled to Spain on Amin's death.   This versio
has the merit of according with Amin's reputation of carin
only for wine, women and song, and also fitting the chronology
for Ziryab arrived in Andalusia in 821: Harun al-Rashid die
in 809, and was succeeded by Amin, who was unwise enough t
ignore the provisions of his will, which gave Khurasan t
Amin's brother Ma'mun, and even to destroy the document
which had been laid up in the sacred Kaaba. Ma'mun a
once established himself in Khurasan, and at the end of fou
years Amin had been defeated by his brother's generals and hi
head sent to him. Ma'mun remained at Merv for severa
years, only coming to Bagdad in 819, when his real reign com
mences, one of the most brilliant in the annals of the Caliphate
It was in all probability the news of his approach that decided
Ziryab to seek fortune elsewhere.

It is a pity that the interests of historical accuracy should
spoil Dozy's story: on the other hand we are allowed to retain
Flecker's conception of an Ishaq less practical and tenderer and
worthier of the lovely words the poet puts in his mouth. As fo
Ziryab, another calamity awaited him at the end of his journey
as he landed at Algeciras he learnt that Hakam, who had
invited him, had just died.   For once his confidence in his sta
deserted him: he was on the point of returning to Africa, but a
humble colleague, a Jew with the odd name of Mansur, en
couraged him with the assurance that Hakam's successor Abd
al-Rahman was an even more generous patron of the arts than
his father.

So indeed it turned out; the new Amir sent a caravan o
mules to fetch him and his household, and instructed the
Governors on his road to show him honours befitting his attain
ments; and when he arrived at Cordoba, the sovereign rode
out to welcome him and accompanied him to the mansion
he had prepared for him.   After three days of rest, he invited
him to the palace, and before asking him to perform assigned
him a salary of two thousand *dinars* a month, with four annual
"benefits"—a thousand *dinars* on the occasion of the two grea

[1] In "Iftitah al-Andalus," translated by Julian Ribera.

feasts of the Sacrifice and the Breaking of the Fast, and five hundred each for Nawruz and Mihrajan. He also made over the revenues of properties worth forty thousand *dinars* and an annual supply of corn and barley for his domestic needs. Only after he had accepted these princely emoluments did he let him sing.

From that moment the Amir took him to his heart, spending hours with him every day not only in listening to his songs (of which Maqqari says he knew a thousand with their tunes, a greater number than Ptolemy who established rules for music), but in discussing history, poetry, art and science, astronomy and geography; for Ziryab was a Pico de la Mirandola who took all knowledge for his province. He entertained the Amir with stories out of a prodigious memory; he became to all intents and purposes one of the royal family, dining with the Amir (who also invited his grown-up sons and made them a separate allowance), and even receiving a key to the palace.

In addition to all these accomplishments he had the priceless gift of tact and charm, which enabled him to spend the rest of his life in perfect serenity as the arbiter of elegances of a court where a foreign intruder could hardly hope to escape intrigue and jealousy. Never before or after, says Maqqari, was a man so universally popular and admired: kings and great ones modelled themselves on him. He was gifted with penetration and wit, profoundly versed in polite literature and infinitely entertaining.

He founded a school of singing, which he conducted with the help of his son Abd al-Rahman, who had inherited his talent. Admission to this academy was conditional on passing a stiff examination, and what we know of the Ziryab method makes it clear that the road to success was thorny. The student was made to sit on a cushion and wind his turban tightly round his middle, which by compressing the diaphragm contributed to the production of a powerful and sustained note. Less obvious is the doctrine that underlay the injunction to sleep with a thick wooden wedge between the jaws: it reminds me of the practice of old-fashioned Turkish singers, who appeared to dislocate their lower jaws at will, while stuffing their right thumb into their ear.

There are few achievements beyond the compass of a film star, and clearly Ziryab enjoyed that status. Anyone who has watched successive generations of young women moulding themselves on Greta Garbo, Marlene Dietrich and Audrey

Hepburn will learn without surprise that Ziryab imposed a new *coiffure* on the adoring multitude: except that the multitude was male. Till his time men wore their hair parted in the middle, with an elf-lock between the eye and the ear. After Ziryab everyone who was anyone wore the "page cut" associated in later centuries with Joan of Arc and Ingrid Bergman; and at that time with eunuchs and concubines. Yet such was his ascendancy, that sober citizens summoned their barbers, and contemplated hesitant reflections in the mirror.

Less perilous was his *fiat* that from Saint John's Day to the 1st October the only wear was white; on the feast of Mihrajan the coloured winter garment had to be flung into the fire of summer. There was however a concession for spring and autumn: for the former *demi-saison* unlined vests were correct, and after October 1st one might quilt one's summer wear with an eye on the chilly mornings.

He also introduced a number of Persian refinements into the toilet, including what may have been a deodorant, and added new lustre to the sovereign's appearance by adding salt to the rose-water in which the royal garments were washed. On the culinary side he was no less resourceful: he was the first to discern the vitue of the asparagus that grew wild in Andalusia; he created *apéritifs* such as *rissoles* and a triangle of pastry fried in oil of coriander seed, besides a dish of which the recipe has not been preserved, *fritto misto alla Ziryab*. Maqqari credits him with teaching the fashionable to drink out of glass instead of plate, and to serve their meals on linen cloths. The leather-workers of Cordoba had cause to be grateful to him for introducing the use of their supple wares for cloaks and table-cloths and beds. But the achievement that brought him lasting fame wherever eastern music is heard was his invention of the fifth string of the lute.

The Arabic mind has a strong bent to mathematics, and it is asserted by some that the relation of notes and numbers at the base of harmonics was well known in Semitic countries long before Pythagoras experimented with the blacksmith's hammers. The Arabic revival of interest in musical theory seems however to have been touched off by translations of works of Greek masters or at least attributed to them: Pythagoras, Plato, Euclid and Aristotle, most of them made under the inspiration of that Ma'mun, whose arrival at Bagdad set Ziryab off on his long journey to Spain. The flood of Arabic works on music is after Ziryab's time, though in his old age he may have known the first Andalusian writer, ibn Firnas:[1] he was no theoretician, but it just came to him like that other

> Fancy's child,
> Warbling his native wood-notes wild;

and his improvement of the lute may fairly be taken as a work of inspiration rather than arithmetic. He certainly thought so and gave his string the name of the "soul". It was the third, says Ribera: the first two were made of silk spun in cold water and highly strung; the others of cat-gut, but the cat was a lion cub, and the tone deeper and more melodious. He believed that the Muses or the Jann taught him new airs as he slept, and kept a couple of slave-girls named Ghazalan and Hinda in his chamber, trained to take down from dictation the compositions distilled from the middle air, that had come to him in his dreams.

Ziryab's name sets a problem in ornithology. Some kind of a bird, without question; Garcia Gomez calls him "*Pájaro Negro*", a black bird, but not *the* blackbird. Maqqari says that Ziryab is a kind of bird like the *zurraiq*, which has a quick understanding, is easy to teach, surpassing the parrot in memory and clearness of diction: those that hear it take it for a man. My dictionary, which is not as good as it should be, translates *zurraiq* by crow or jay—two birds scarcely identical. The triliteral root z r q means blue or grey: other derivatives are translated "falcon" and "white sparrow hawk". None of these birds seems right, and I am tempted by "starling" which is *zurzur* in Arabic—a quite different radical. Colour, like taste, is a subject on which discussion is ruled out: one cannot do better than follow Garcia Gomez, which will allow us to write Ziryab's epitaph

Rara avis in terris, nigroque simillima cycno.

[1] Abu Qasim Abbas ibn Firnas was another remarkable product of Cordoba: poet, musician, astronomer, mechanician and even airman. He discovered a process of extracting glass from sand, invented the metronome and constructed a working orrery. According to the testimony of several trustworthy authors, says Maqqari, he covered himself with feathers and put on a pair of wings, flying a certain distance and returning to his starting point. Unfortunately he made a bad landing, having failed to study the braking effect of a bird's tail.

IBN AMMAR, THE POET WHO WOULD BE KING
(11th century)

If you have found your way to Praia da Rocha, thirty-odd miles east of Cape Saint Vincent (and a blessed little beach if only the travel agents leave it alone), it is a very short run to Silves, a quiet little township now, with Arab ramparts and a Gothic church, surrounded by a rich plain, with cornland, orchards and market gardens. Nothing worth an asterisk in the guide-books; the people are just the pleasant folk you have been meeting ever since you came to Portugal. There is no particular reason why you should make the expedition, unless you wanted to capture the charm that left so deep an imprint on the youthful Mu'tamid.

In his time, nine hundred odd years ago, Silves was the capital of the district of Algarve, in the dominions of the Banu Abbad, the successors of the Caliphate, and was a fitting command for the young heir to the throne to try his wings. It was there that he met the poet ibn Ammar, who played a dominant part in his life.

Abu Bakr ibn Ammar was a native of Shannabus, in the department of Silves: he came of a poor and obscure family. He learnt his letters at Silves, which at the time was famous as a sort of Arcadia, where everybody spoke in verse; he went on to more advanced studies at Cordoba, keeping soul and body alive by the manufacture of poetry. He travelled over all Andalus, paying for board and lodging with an ode, but never accumulating enough to fit himself out with a decent suit of clothes. Wherever he went, he used to excite derision with his poverty-stricken get-up, but they had to applaud the quality of his verse. His gipsy wanderings had a happy ending when he met Mu'tadid, the Abbadi king of Seville, and conquered him with a famous *qasida*, which begins

"Send round the cup, for the morning breeze freshens and the Pleiads have ended their nightly journey:
Whatever touches Mu'tadid's hand grows green, as the world puts on its fresh mantle:
The flint of glory only lets the fire of war die down in order to kindle the fire of hospitality:
If he gives a maid, he chooses one with swelling bosoms: if a horse, a thoroughbred: if a sword, then it is jewelled."

And much more to the same purpose. Mu'tadid gave him the robes and horse and money that he had so long hankered after, and entered him on the roll of his salaried poets. He soon made the acquaintance of the young prince, and conquered him entirely. "His situation did not cease from increasing, until Mu'tamid esteemed him like the apples of his eyes, and could not be separated from his friend, day or night." When his father sent him as Governor to Silves, he took ibn Ammar along with him as principal adviser, "and he had the most absolute sovereignty over him".

Some unromantic authorities maintain that the association was vicious, but so far as I can see, they base their opinion on nothing more cogent than the fact that that kind of *amitié amoureuse* was not rare in Andalus, nor particularly frowned on. I would myself like to give Mu'tamid the benefit of the doubt, because he had many virtues as well as failings: it is too easy to argue that an exquisite poet is unlikely to be a normal man; he was however in his later life a man of his hands, who gave a good account of himself in the *mêlée*. We have all had the junior school tailing after us when we were prefects and had half a dozen colours, and Mu'tamid's *envoûtement* at thirteen was very likely just a romantic adoration for a brilliant man ten years his senior.

The father however took the plain man's view, and banished ibn Ammar to the other end of the kingdom, and he spent weary years at Zaragoza as long as Mu'tadid reigned; Mu'tamid brought him back as soon as he succeeded, and "took him into his closest confidence, associating him with matters with which no man associates his father or brother". The chronicler shows his disapproval, but he was writing after the event and to point a moral.

The new King gave ibn Ammar the choice of any office in the kingdom, and must have been a little dashed when, instead of opting for a post in the capital, where he would be near Mu'tamid, he plumped for the governorship of Silves, in order to have his revenge for all the slights he had had to endure during his youth. A sad *parvenu*, I fear, but he was only allowed a very short time to indulge his spite, before Mu'tamid called him to Cordoba, appointed him *wazir* and showed him every kind of honour: in particular inviting him to every one of his literary *symposia*, at which they

"tired the sun with talking and sent him down the sky."

One such night, when he had kept him at the palace, he had a nightmare: three times a voice awakened him, saying "Beware! one day this man will take thy life". The third time he got up and crept to the palace door, intending to rise as soon as it was opened, take ship to Africa and hide among the Berbers: in the meantime he wrapped himself in a carpet to wait for dawn.   Mu'tamid however saw his empty couch, and organized a search, discovering him huddled in his mat, sobbing hysterically.   When ibn Ammar stammered out the reason for his distress, the king's eyes filled with tears, and he cried, "How could I slay thee, who art my life?   The fumes of wine have darkened thy counsel: forget these cursed dreams and never speak of them again."   Ibn Ammar recovered his assurance, and came to forget his nightmare; but in the end his presentiment was realized.

Of his talents there can be no question; it was not only out of regard for a brother poet that Mu'tamid entrusted him with his most important missions.   Indeed Marraqushi says that whatsoever was put before him he resolved efficiently and marked it with his seal, as if it were iron reddened in the fire. He was renowned all over Spain, and even Alfonso VI, who was steadily increasing his pressure on the Taifas, judged him the most eminent man in the peninsula.   Alfonso had frequent dealings with him, both as associate and adversary, and had taken his measure.   Once when Alfonso was marching southwards at the head of a considerable force, and Cordoba lay open and all but defenceless, ibn Ammar secured a respite by a famous trick.   He owned a set of chessmen, so marvellously wrought that no king had the like.   The pieces were of ebony and sandal-wood inlaid with gold, and the board was a marvel of joinery.   With this in his baggage he went to meet the Christian at the frontier: Alfonso received him with every mark of courtesy, bidding his courtiers repair to his tent and see that he lacked for nothing.   The chessmen were exhibited to his visitors, who at once reported to Alfonso, a keen exponent of the game.   At the ceremonial reception, he asked if he played: ibn Ammar answered that he did, "and indeed he was most proficient".   Alfonso then asked to see the chessmen, but ibn Ammar only consented to show them on condition that they had a match, the stakes to be the chessmen against a wish, if ibn Ammar won.   "They brought the set and showed it to the King, who exclaimed, crossing himself, 'Never had I believed chessmen could be so perfect.'   Then he turned to ibn Ammar, and asked, 'What was thy word?'   The Muslim repeated his conditions; Alfonso refused, saying, 'I know not what thou mayst ask: it may be something I cannot give.'   Ibn Ammar replied, 'I play only under these conditions,' and began to wrap the pieces up and sent them to his tent.   Nevertheless the *wazir* revealed to certain of the courtiers under pledge of secrecy what he had in mind to ask if he won the match, and assured himself of their aid by the promise of large sums."

As the King was obsessed by desire for the set, his courtiers had little difficulty in persuading him to play.   If he won, the exquisite chessmen were his, while if he lost, what could his adversary ask that a king could not grant?   Moreover they themselves were at hand to make the man see reason.   Alfonso then accepted the challenge, and when he had to acknowledge defeat, ibn Ammar asked that he should leave Mu'tamid's territory and go back to his own.   For a moment the King thought to refuse, but "his company showed him what great shame it would be for the greatest king of the age to betray his oath, and insisted with so much ability that he recovered his calm".   He withdrew accordingly, but got even by demanding twice the customary tribute.   Ibn Ammar hastened to accept, and so "by the prudence and sagacity of the *wazir*, Allah sheltered the Muslims from the violence of the Polytheists, and ibn Ammar went back to his lord, who was delighted by so happy an event".

The poet-wazir's successes turned his head completely, and no doubt the affectionate treatment he always received from his master led him to underrate his quality.   "Led astray by pride and yielding to the temptations of Satan," he began to caress dreams of a throne for himself, and set himself to achieve his ambition with the cold-blooded technique of a Talleyrand. There were three outstanding kings in Spain—Alfonso, Mu'tamid and Abd Allah, king of Granada; the last wrote his memoirs, which Lévi-Provençal has translated.   They show how ibn Ammar played them off against one another, with the steady purpose of picking up a kingdom for himself out of the confusion.

His chance came when Mu'tamid, who still had faith in him, sent him to round off his dominions in the east by the capture of Murcia, promising to leave him there as governor, if he succeeded.   There was little advantage to be gained from the possession of a town even more exposed to Christian enterprise than Seville or Cordoba, and liable at any time to be cut off by raids from Granada: one sees the hand of ibn Ammar behind the plan; he had chosen his kingdom.

He captured the town, with the complicity of one ibn Rashiq, the lord of a castle commanding the approaches, who had strong partisans within the walls.   The Prince, ibn Tahir, a kindly old gentleman, whom all regretted, was expelled and went to Valencia; ibn Ammar settled in as governor, with ibn Rashiq as his lieutenant. He at once took on the airs of a sovereign, treated direct with the Almoravid sultan in Africa and had his name substituted for Mu'tamid's in the Friday sermon. Mu'tamid remonstrated—in verse: ibn Ammar replied in the same metre: the poetic exchange became heated, till the infatuated poet sent off an unforgivable *qasida* reflecting on Mu'tamid's beloved wife Rumaiqiyya and their sons. That was the beginning of the end.

Ibn Ammar, now King of Murcia in his own estimation, soon felt himself impelled to expand his kingdom at the expense of Valencia, and set off at the head of a small force to reconnoitre. As soon as he was out of sight, ibn Rashiq, who had his own ambitions, and a native party to put them into effect, seized power and closed the gates against ibn Ammar, who suddenly found himself without a friend. Unable to return to Cordoba, he took the disconsolate path to Zaragoza, where he had passed the dreary years of exile. The king, who knew of his disloyalty to Mu'tamid, gave him a chilly welcome, and he had to continue his round of visits, finding none to take him in. Finally, in a desperate effort to win favour, he undertook to capture the stronghold of Segura by one of his famous *ruses de guerre*, but was himself captured and put into chains. His captor, ibn Mubarak, was uncertain what to do with him, till ibn Ammar, with a sort of perverted pride, suggested putting him up to auction among the princes, many of whom would be glad to pay a stiff price for him. He was impelled to put the matter into verse:

"One morning they brought me to the market, and men made divers bids for my head:
I call Allah to witness that whoever paid the price had value for his money."

Mu'tamid bought him in and haled him back to Cordoba under strong escort. As they came in sight of the city, he gave fresh proof, says Marraqushi, of the vivacity of his intuition. A horseman came spurring to meet them; as he saw him, ibn Ammar began to unwind his turban. He knew, none better, that the 'procession of shame' awaited him, a favourite punishment for crimes like his. He was paraded through the town bare-headed and loaded with chains, perched on a mule between two sacks of straw; the whole population was ordered into the streets to gloat over his ignominy. "Instead of princes

nd notables jostling for the privilege of kissing his hand, he
ntered the city despised, timorous and destitute, with nothing
is except the garments he wore. Glory to Allah," says
Marraqushi, "who despoiled him of the gifts he had granted
im, and deprived him of that that he had permitted him to
njoy."

He had to endure the same degradation at Seville and was
hen thrown into a dungeon at Mu'tamid's palace. From
here he bombarded the King with *qasidas* expressing his
emorse and begging for forgiveness.

Once at least he touched Mu'tamid's heart; he granted him
n interview and recited to him all the favours he had received:
on Ammar made no reply, but embraced his feet and wetted
hem with his tears. He extracted a half-promise of forgive-
ess, but his essential *hubris* was too much for him. He had
egged two sheets of paper to make a copy of the poem that had
oftened his master; he used the second to write to one of
Mu'tamid's sons that he had pulled it off, and would soon be
ut of prison. The letter was delivered during the Prince's
rtulia and read aloud. Some of his enemies were present,
who, when they learnt the news, spread it about, adding
nfamies which I will not relate". This was too much:
Mu'tamid caught up a double-axe, which lay close to his hand,
nd rushed down to his cell. Ibn Ammar crawled to him and
mbraced his feet, "but he struck him with the axe and stayed
ot his hand, till he was cold". Then when his rage was spent,
e had the body washed and shrouded and buried in the
3lessed Palace.

IBN ABDUN, THE CENSOR
(12th century)

Among the pompous Arabic texts from which we derive our
knowledge of the Caliphate of Cordoba, few condescend to
lescribe the way of life of the ordinary people: the subject is
peneath the notice of the elegant historian, whose polished
periods are devoted to sovereigns, poets and law-givers, whenever they are not confined to natural science or abstract
peculation. There are however two short works that stand
ut from the ruck of refined and insipid narrative and offer a
vivid picture of the everyday life of the great cities of Muslim
3pain.

By a coincidence—if indeed it is one—both authors wrote at
he end of the 11th century, and both treat of the administration

of a town, cataloguing the officers who preside over the town
people's concerns, the mosques, the schools, the markets, th
guilds, the water-supply and such routine matters, and layin
down rules for their governance.   Both texts were discovere
and published by the late Professor Lévi-Provençal, and on
Ibn Abdun al-Tujibi's treatise on Seville, has been translate
into Spanish by Professor Garcia Gomez: the other, al-Sakati
manual on Malaga, still awaits a rendering into a Europea
language.   The delay arises out of deference to the Frenc
savant's claim to the rights of translation of texts discovered b
him: Professor Garcia Gomez's scruple led him to wait for
French translation by Lévi-Provençal before publishing hi
own version of ibn Abdun: unfortunately Lévi-Provençal'
failure to carry out his promise to publish a French version c
al-Sakati has prevented others from translating more than
few extracts for a quarter of a century.

It is surprising that ibn Abdun at Seville and al-Sakati a
Malaga should have hit on so unusual a theme at the sam
moment: perhaps one may conjecture that the Almoravi
rulers, feeling the need of advice on the government of thei
new and outlandish subjects, had circularized their provincia
governors, calling for suggestions from local experts, and tha
they had elicited a number of responses, of which these are th
only survivors.   Whether this is a good guess or no, there is n
question of their interest: the two treatises provide a livel
account of the life of the people; in the words of Garcia Gomez
ibn Abdun opens a window on to the teeming market
place of Seville, its silent mosque and magnificent river: whil
al-Sakati, so far as may be judged from the few extracts tha
have been published, is no less racy and revealing.

Nothing is known of ibn Abdun beyond what may be deduce
from internal evidence.   A *faqih* undoubtedly: a stern Puritan
an Andalusian with no great affection for the veiled conqueror
that stalk through his native streets, and the uncivilized Berber
of their armies: an official himself, one would say, in one of th
services which he sets out to regulate: perhaps even a qadi o
almotacen, according to Lévi-Provençal, though his book offer
little suggestion of such eminence: a man with both feet on th
ground, who did his own shopping and was up to all the device
of tradesmen and artisans, police and tax-gatherers and lawyers
even of judges and *wazirs*: armed with a poor opinion o
women, a profound distrust of all men and a limitless aversio
to young bachelors.   With all this pessimism he was stil
capable of compassion; he can draft humane regulations for th

isons, and think of providing benches in the ablution rooms
the mosques, covered with the discarded carpets, so that the
estitute may get a night's sleep.

His motive in writing, he says, is his sincere affection for the
Muslims (whom God preserve!) and his desire to give them good
dvice, to confirm their estate and improve their condition, to
ncourage them to seek and find the good, and to know and
llow justice. To repress injustice and tyranny is an integral
art of the struggle against evil: "may God defend us from
ebellion against his laws, vouchsafe us a good end in this world
nd the next, and protect us with his grace and loving aid
gainst all that should be avoided. Amen."

After this pious exordium, he proceeds to define the ideal
rince, probably having in mind the Almoravid governor of the
rovince, and the line of conduct to be followed by his advisers.
Ie is the brain of his people, the axis of the body politic and as it
vere the middle point of a circle, whose perfection and symmetry depend on the stability of its centre. The men of wisdom
nust watch over him and correct any aberration or short-
omings: if he is hard and violent, they must tactfully bring
im to a better judgment, by dwelling on the impermanency
f human affairs, exemplified by historical analogies, and
eminding him of the catastrophes that brought other kingdoms
o nought. Above all, they must bring him to summon the
adi and the *faqihs* and the men of goodwill and to study the
ffairs of his people at first hand. This model prince must
ake an active and intelligent interest in agriculture, which is
he source of wealth and peace, setting his ministers and nobles
o cultivate the soil: so shall they grow rich and the people be
ed. If he does all this, how fortunate he! but where should we
ind such a prince?

From the prince, ibn Abdun passes to the leading officers,
qadi, *zalmedina*, *almotacen*. The capital rôle played by the
qadi is examined in another chapter: if we may trust ibn
Abdun, he had acquired in 12th century Seville powers that he
never had under the Caliphate. The *zalmedina* and *almotacen*
are under his orders: he has a subordinate judge, or *hakim*, to
release him from unimportant cases and contact with the vulgar
herd: the only officer of similar calibre is the *wazir*, who seems
to stand next to the governor in the citadel, but still to be at the
beck and call of the qadi. He must summon the *wazir* morning
and evening to discuss current affairs; if he is amenable, the
two will work in harmony to school the prince. But the qadi
must take care that the *wazir* does not take an independent line

M

with the governor, and if he has two faces, must lose no tin
in getting him dismissed. It is a good scheme to sham illne
and get the governor to visit him in his house: so shall h
reputation be exalted. Finally he should not omit to cultiva
those who might one day replace the great man.

The atmosphere of ibn Abdun's Seville is heavy with intrigu
and suspicion: the qadi has to keep an eye on everyone; h
must call for at least a monthly audit of the accounts of th
waqfs, in case of negligence or fraud: his own *hakim*, for all h
guarantees of wealth and breeding and legal training an
integrity, will still bear watching: the tax-assessors are shame
less liars and swindlers: as for the advocates, it would be bette
to suppress them altogether, because all their study is to mak
people waste their money and to procure unjust verdicts. A
they cannot be dispensed with altogether, he must choose ther
as nearly honourable as possible, not open to bribes or wine
bibbers or libertines or even young, but never trust them wit
the defence of a woman, because at once they would set abou
seducing her, and keep the case pending so as to continue in th
enjoyment of her favours. The court ushers are just as bad
above all one must beware of young ones; if allowed t
approach a woman, the first thing they would do would be t
rape or seduce her.

Ibn Abdun's picture of his contemporaries is a little dispirit
ing, because his primary object is to put down abuses: it is n
part of his programme to award prizes for good conduct
There is no reason to doubt that he knew his Seville, and tha
the iniquities he describes flourished there, as in other capital
before and since. Miguel Asin Palacios, one of the grea
authorities on Muslim Spain, speaks of contemporary Cordoba
as the "*cloaca maxima* where debauch and the grossest sensuality
discharged their filth", and Cordoba was always accounted
more enlightened than Seville, which was rarely praised for
anything but merriment and high spirits—the last thing to
appeal to ibn Abdun.

When he comes to discuss the *ferias* and *fiestas* that seem never
to have been wanting in Seville, he gives free rein to his disgust
They are a great occasion of stumbling, he says, far too often
attended by those youths and bachelors. At all times soldiers
and *alguaciles* must be after them, for they are too often
criminals, thieves and malefactors, particularly during the
summer, when everyone is in the fields. Music too has the
worst effect on their youthful humours; and although unfortunately musicians cannot be completely liquidated, they

must not be allowed into the countryside without a permit from the qadi, who will despatch sufficient *alguaciles* to prevent the *fiesta* becoming a riot. As for those naughty bachelors, they must be constrained to do the field work, and their fathers who brought them up so badly are to be held responsible for their misdoings. One of the marks of the contemporary Teddy-boy was long hair; wherefore if one was caught with a lance, which in conjunction with long hair was enough to lead him into unrighteousness, it must at once be taken from him, and his head shaved.[1] Ibn Abdun's account of these detrimentals has features familiar to the English employer of labour to-day. "One of them agrees for a day's work at a fixed rate for so many hours, and abandons his work before the time, and idles with no sense of his duties, spends an hour gathering wood or washing himself or satisfying a need, but not working; and then comes to you at the close of the day as if he had done everything that he undertook, magnifying the services he has rendered, and complaining that the recompense is not adequate." To say nothing of their dissolute behaviour in the cemeteries, hanging about among the graves to take advantage of the widows and mourners!

So much went on in the cemeteries, which were the only public breathing-spaces in the overcrowded rabbit-warren of 12th century Seville. The broad gardens of the Alcazar belonged to the prince and his familiars: the great mosque where the Cathedral now stands, with its Patio de los Naranjos, was only built a century later: the existing mosque, now the church of San Salvador, was miserably inadequate: the only place of recreation was an open field outside the north walls of the town. The cemeteries were insufficient for their proper service: the dead were buried on top of the earlier tenants of the graves, and the grave-diggers were so set on economizing space that sometimes the corpse was literally fitted with his grave, being taken out twice or thrice while a little more earth was scooped out, till he could lie at ease. What was worse, people used to sit on the tombs to commit all sorts of wickedness: they even installed latrines which ran over the dead Muslims. Some wretches had gone so far as to build booths, which Mu'tamid had had demolished when he began to reign, but all were back again. The cemeteries must be patrolled

---

[1] The same view of the connection between hair and sin used to obtain at Oxford, where among other prohibitions and injunctions freshmen were forbidden to grow excessive hair—*ne nutriant inordinatas comas*—and also restrained from playing marbles on the Senate House steps.

twice a day, in particular the fenced areas round certain *turbes*, which on hot days during the *siesta* hours were transformed into so many brothels. No hawkers should be allowed in: they were less concerned to sell their wares than to catch women unveiled; no fortune-tellers either, and even the man who recites the Quran at funerals must not be a bachelor, not even if he is blind.

When ibn Abdun comes to legislate for the mosques, his directions are so complete as to suggest that he had practical experience of their working: he lays down a minimum of three servants, two to sweep, one for the water, the last to be provided with a donkey to fetch the skins between the midday and the afternoon prayers. There must be a mason permanently employed in the upkeep of the fabric; the approaches are to be kept clear of stalls; copper-smiths and tinkers have to close down during the prayers: the hawkers in the courtyard must sweep it clean on Friday mornings, and take themselves off till after the midday prayers. No beggars, no horses, no armed men, no children with dirty shoes. And there must be as many extra *muezzins* as there were doors, so that the worshippers who were unable to push their way into the overcrowded mosque could take their time from him, to make their prostrations in unison with the prayer-leader inside.

With the town bursting at the seams, the Christians seem to have been pushed out across the river to the Triana suburb, where they have now been succeeded by the gypsies; there they plied their trades and produced their abhorrent but so delicious wares. Ibn Abdun makes no secret of his hatred of Christians and Jews: their church bells must be silenced, and a good Muslim must not give them the *salaam*. At a pinch they may be employed as *masseurs* in the baths, or scavengers or muckmen, but they must not dress like decent *bourgeois*, nor sell their old clothes—a disability shared with libertines and lepers. Nor must they be allowed to read books of science, nor practise as doctors to the Muslims; how can they be relied on?

There was as yet no bridge across the river, so communication depended on watermen, whose rascally tricks did not escape ibn Abdun's keen eye. They must not overload their boats, above all in gusty weather, nor let their passengers row, nor ferry any of those blacks and Berbers who habitually made free of other folks' property; indeed no notorious pilferer or drunkard, no harlot, and finally none of those reprobate Muslims who carried demijohns to Triana, to fill them with the infidels' wine.

Ibn Abdun had a tenderness for the Guadalquivir, which was the very life-blood of Seville; he will brook no building on the banks, which must be kept free and accessible to all: the washerwomen must keep away from the upper reaches, where the drinking-water was drawn: no-one was to discharge rubbish from the banks—but I cannot believe that any Andalusian ever respected that injunction. And I am surprised that ibn Abdun, who missed so little, should not have censured that intense traffic on the river during the warm summer nights, when everyone was out in countless little boats with their lanterns, carrying pleasure-seekers in every direction with those unholy lutes and demijohns, exchanging songs and *coplas* and who knows what unseemly banter? One can hardly suppose that he countenanced such proceedings: he must have been safely in bed in his own patio.

BIBLIOGRAPHY

P. Agrado Bleye, "Manual de Historia de España," Madrid, 1954

Akhbar Majmu'a, translated by E. Lafuente Alcántara, Madrid 1867.

R. Altamira, "Historia de España y de la civilizacion Española," Barcelona, 1911.

M. Asin Palacios, "Abenhazam de Cordoba y su Historia critica de las ideas religiosas," vols. I to V, Madrid, 1927-32.
"El Islam cristianizado," Madrid, 1931.
"Huellas del Islam," Madrid, 1941.

Americo Castro, "España en su Historia, Cristianos, Moros y Judios," Buenos Ayres, 1948.

Cresswell, "Early Muslim Architecture," Oxford, 1940.

Charles Diehl, in "Glotz's Histoire du Moyen Age," Vol. III.

Reinhart Dozy, "le Calendrier de Cordoue de l'année 961" (Rabi' ibn Zaid) Leyden, 1873.
"Histoire des Musulmans d'Espagne jusqu'a la conquête de l'Andalousie par les Almohades," 4 vols., Leyden, 1861. Revised and brought up to date by Lévi-Provençal, Leyden, 1931.
"Recherches sue l'histoire et la littérature de l'Espagne pendant le Moyen Age," Leyden, 1881.

Emilio Garcia Gomez, "Cinco Poetas Musulmanos," Madrid, 1943.
"El Collar de la Paloma de ibn Hazm de Cordoba," Madrid, 1952.
"Elogio del Islam Español (al-Shaqundi)," Madrid, 1934.
"Poemas Arabigo-andaluces," Madrid,
"Silla del Moro," Madrid, 1948.

P. de Gayangos, "The History of the Mohammedan Dynasties in Spain (al-Maqqari)," London, 1840-3.

A. Gonzalez Palencia, "El Islam y Occidente," Madrid, 1931.
"Historia de la España Musulmana," Madrid, 1932.

A. Guillaume, "Islam," London, 1954.

Ibn Adhari, "Bayan al-Mughrib," translation by E. Fagnan, Algiers 1901-4. Completed by Lévi-Provençal, Paris, 1930.

"The Legacy of Islam" (Sir Thomas Arnold and Alfred Guillaume), Oxford, 1952.

"The Legacy of Israel," Oxford, 1953.

E. Lévi-Provençal, "L'Espagne Musulmane au 10e siécle," Paris, 1932.
"Histoire de l'Espagne musulmane," 1931–1953.
"Les Mémoires de Abd Allah, dernier roi Ziride de Grenade,"
"La Civilizacion Arabe en España," Buenos Ayres, 1953.
"La Péninsule Ibérique au Moyen Age d'après le Kitab el Rawd el Mi'tar fi Habar al Aktar de ... Himyari," Leyden, 1948-1951.
"Séville Musulmane au début du 12e siécle; le traité d'ibn Abdun," 1948. Spanish version in collaboration by E. Garcia Gomez, "Sevilla musulmana a comienzos del Siglo XII," Madrd, 1948.

A. Mez, "Renacimiento del Islam" (Vila's translation), Madrid, 1936.

J. C. Murphy, "History of the Mahometan Empire in Spain," 1816.

H. Pérès, "La Poésie Andalouse du 11e Siécle en Arabe Classique," Madrid, 1928.

Julian Ribera, "Disertaciones y Opusculos," Madrid, 1928.
"Historia de la Conquista de España de Abenalcotia el Cordobes ..." Madrid, 1926.
"La Música de las Cantigas," Madrid, 1922.
"Historia de los Jueces de Cordoba (al-Khushani)," Madrid, 1914.

C. Sanchez Albornoz, "La España Musulmana," Buenos Ayres, 1946.

F. Simonet, "Historia de los Mozarabes de España," Madrid, 1903.

L. Torres Balbas, "La Mezquita de Cordoba y Madinat al-Zahra," Madrid, 1952.

R. Velazquez Bosco, "Medina Azzahra y Alamiriya," Madrid, 1912.

Periodicals: "al-Andalus," Madrid and Granada.

INDEX

W

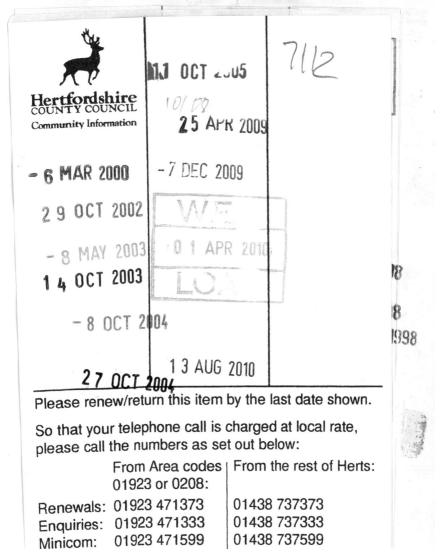

Hertfordshire
COUNTY COUNCIL
Community Information

Please renew/return this item by the last date shown.

So that your telephone call is charged at local rate,
please call the numbers as set out below:

	From Area codes 01923 or 0208:	From the rest of Herts:
Renewals:	01923 471373	01438 737373
Enquiries:	01923 471333	01438 737333
Minicom:	01923 471599	01438 737599

L32